Contents

Introduction

Aims of the guide

The purpose of this Student Text Guide to Jane Austen's *Pride and Prejudice* is to enable you to organise your thoughts and responses to the novel, to deepen your understanding of key features and aspects, and finally to help you to address the particular requirements of examination questions in order to obtain the best possible grade. It will also prove useful to those writing a coursework piece on the novel by providing a number of summaries, lists, analyses and references to help with the content and construction of the assignment.

It is assumed that you have read and studied the novel already under the guidance of a teacher or lecturer. This is a revision guide, not an introduction to the text, although some of its content serves the purpose of providing initial background. It can be read in its entirety in one sitting, or it can be dipped into and used as a reference guide to specific and separate aspects of the novel.

The remainder of this *Introduction* consists of an overview of the Assessment Objectives, which summarise the requirements of the schemes of assessment employed by the various exam boards.

The *Text Guidance* consists of a series of subsections that examine key aspects of the text, including contexts, interpretations and controversies. Terms defined in 'Literary terms and concepts' are highlighted the first time they appear in this section.

The final section, *Questions and Answers*, gives extensive practical advice about writing the various types of essay answer, and includes mark schemes, model essay plans and some examples of marked work.

Note that the examiners are seeking above all else evidence of an *informed personal response* to the text. A revision guide such as this can help you to understand the text and to form your own opinions, and can suggest areas to think about it, but it cannot replace your own ideas and responses as an individual reader.

Assessment Objectives

The revised Assessment Objectives for A-level English Literature from 2008 are common to all boards:

AO1	articulate creative, informed and relevant responses to literary texts, using appropriate terminology and concepts, and coherent, accurate written expression

AO2	demonstrate detailed critical understanding in analysing the ways in which structure, form and language shape meanings in literary texts
AO3	explore connections and comparisons between different literary texts, informed by interpretations of other readers
AO4	demonstrate understanding of the significance and influence of the contexts in which literary texts are written and received

Text Guidance

Contexts

Life and works of Jane Austen

The Austen family

The family of six boys and two girls was not an unusually large one, but it was atypical in that they all survived childhood. Mrs Austen's practice was to farm out her babies to a village woman to nurse between the ages of 3 and 18 months. However, George, the mentally ill brother, 'was never able to take his place in the family' (R. W. Chapman); being locked away was the normal treatment for mental illness at the time. Jane was sent away to school but nearly died of a fever, and she returned home with Cassandra when she was nine. Jane was devoted to and influenced by her elder sister of three years, and like her she never married, though four of her five brothers did. It is believed that Cassandra may well have influenced Jane's rejection of her one offer of marriage in order to keep her sister to herself.

To supplement their income, the Austen parents took in boy boarders, and these, in addition to the six brothers of her own, made the young Jane, like her *Northanger Abbey* heroine Catherine Morland, familiar with boys' games and pre-occupations; this familiarity shows in her early writings and accounts for the ferocious boyish humour and word play, the unkind comments, the cheerful violence, and the lack of sentimentality, for example towards ugly females and babies. One brother, Francis, rose in the navy from midshipman to admiral; Henry is said to have been her favourite brother; her brother James was a published writer in his own magazine, *The Loiterer* (1789–91). We hear little about her mother, also Cassandra, although she was a writer of humorous verses and had aristocratic and academic relatives. She was also, however, a hypochondriac, a condition that Jane borrowed and mocked in her portrayal of both Mr Woodhouse in *Emma* and Mrs Bennet. Her father encouraged Jane's literary aspirations, ensuring that she always had writing paper, which was then an expensive luxury item.

In 1790, when she was 14, the family became enthusiastic about amateur theatricals (though they are much disapproved of in *Mansfield Park*). The fact that in Austen's novels language is primarily a spoken rather than a written medium, and that she had a finely tuned ear for social **dialogue** and nuance, can be attributed to the family's habit of reading novels and their own offerings out loud to each other. She wrote to give advice on writing to her niece Fanny Knight, and five of those letters survive. Biographical family details appear in her novels: for instance the topaz crosses sent to her and Cassandra by their brother Charles feature in *Mansfield Park*; Marianne's near death from a putrid throat in *Sense and Sensibility* was her own experience; marriages between cousins occurred among her own family members as well as in her fiction. Family memoirs are contradictory, claiming that Austen was proper and reserved but also charming, loved and feared, biting of tongue but tender of heart. However, these same complexities of character are apparent in the novels, and could be said to be particularly true of Elizabeth Bennet.

In addition to being one of eight children, Austen had a large quantity of cousins, spread across many counties and even beyond the shores of England. Her sister-in-law Eliza, who eventually married brother Henry, lost her former husband, a count, to the guillotine in France in 1794. Her nephew James Edward Austen-Leigh, who wrote about her in 1870, tells us that according to family recollections Jane met in a southern seaside town a clergyman whom she might have married if he had not died. Cassandra was betrothed to a reverend who died of yellow fever in the West Indies in 1797, so Jane was copying her sister's experience in this as in so much else. At Christmas in 1796 Jane met Tom Lefroy, her 'Irish friend', with whom she fell in love. He admitted as an old man and as Lord Chief Justice of Ireland that he had loved her too.

In 1802 Cassandra and Jane visited Steventon, now held as a living by their brother James. Harris Bigg-Wither, son of a neighbouring county family, there proposed to Jane, who accepted but then had doubts and changed her mind overnight. She thus became one of the most famous maiden aunts in English history. In 1808 she looked after the sons of Edward (her third brother), whose mother had just died. Edward had been on a grand tour after being adopted by wealthy relations, a common practice at the time, as featured in *Mansfield Park*.

As with the Brontë sisters, having a clergyman father was the way in which daughters could get to be considered gentry despite limited means; they could also expect to be educated beyond the station of most women of the time, as education had elevated their fathers. There were always books to be found in a vicarage that would not otherwise have been readily available, and a habit of study to go with them. Also like the Brontës, Austen was well aware of the subtle shadings of the family's middling social position. Her family rubbed shoulders with both the local village folk and the country gentry, and belonged to the lesser gentry, meaning less wealthy but better educated than the true gentry, which consisted of established county families with extensive property. Except for an eight-year interlude in Bath in her twenties — which she did not enjoy — and a brief sojourn in Southampton, Austen spent her life in the Hampshire countryside, where she embraced Tory but democratic values. In a margin of her copy of Goldsmith's *History* she wrote 'How much are the poor to be pitied, and the Rich to be Blamed'. As Eagleton explains in his essay on Austen in *The English Novel*, 'The English landed gentry was a capitalist class', though one with a 'distinctly Protestant dimension'. He describes Austen as 'a "modern" conservative rather than a Romantic reactionary' who, like Dickens, advocates 'reform and improvement within the status quo', and is both 'an astringent critic and an ardent champion' of rural squirearchy.

Literary influences

Jane was allowed the uncensored use of the 500 volumes in her father's library, and read Samuel Richardson's *Sir Charles Grandison* as a child. She was particularly fond of this work, and Isabella Thorpe's condemnation of it in *Northanger Abbey* as 'an amazing horrid book' is major evidence of Isabella's lack of literary taste. In Richardson's novel there are descriptions of sisters, and particularly one called Charlotte who could be a prototype for the heroine of *Pride and Prejudice* in being high-spirited, teasing, captivating, lively, articulate and arch, with a badly behaved father. There are also other character types and concerns that are reflected in Austen's novel, including a fortune-hunting army officer, 'girls of slender fortunes', and many discussions of love and marriage.

According to Henry, his sister Jane was a precocious reader and 'intimately acquainted with the merits and defects of the best essays and novels in the English language'. He stated in his biographical note that Johnson and Cowper were her favourite 'moral writers'. She admired Johnson's *Rasselas* and his essays in the *Rambler* and the *Idler*, allowing his ironic and measured **style** to influence her own. Cowper's long poem 'The Task' condemned field sports and their cruelty, but because her brothers were so fond of them Austen never openly condemns them in her fiction or surviving letters. She also kept quiet on politics and women's rights (Mary Wollstonecraft's *Vindication of the Rights of Woman* was published to a furore Jane could not have been unaware of in 1792). It seems her staunch Tory background silenced her possible sympathies towards radical sentiments, which she did not dare to endorse publicly out of loyalty to her family and fear of the effect it would have on her literary standing. However, she discreetly satirises hunters and male chauvinists through uncharitable portraits such as that of John Thorpe in *Northanger Abbey*, and her books quietly insist on and illustrate the moral and intellectual parity of the sexes.

Though much was made after her death of her piety, Austen does not overtly refer to religion either; no one prays or has an inner spiritual struggle, and God is rarely mentioned, but Christian precepts of neighbourliness, charity, patience and justice inform the decent social behaviour of every approved-of character in her works as a form of secularised Christianity to be applied to fellow humans. Though there is little scene-setting and material detail in her works, there is a fidelity to the niceties of social interaction and mimetic **realism** of speech within the closed world that she is describing and assessing; what have been described as 'the long shadows of small events in a limited society'. Through what Hough (p. 227) calls 'strongly ideological constructions', 'coherence is attained by a deliberate limitation of possibilities', creating a distinctive moral system still recognised today, and actually still practised until at least the First World War. Eagleton comments on 'her extraordinary moral intelligence'. Although place is important to Austen, as represented in three of her seven novel titles (including *Sanditon*), another three are moral titles; at a time when it was common to choose **eponymous** titles, as Fielding and Richardson did, only *Emma* is a name.

We know from Tomalin (p. 67) that Austen also enjoyed Sterne's playful exposure of literary convention and artifice, and despite not particularly approving of the content of Fielding's works, Austen's own satiric manner of mocking absurdity and pricking pretentiousness of sentiment or social position owes something to him. In addition she read and admired the female writers Fanny Burney, Maria Edgeworth and Charlotte Smith. Her novels reflect the social attitudes of the females of the upper bourgeoisie of her time, but look backward to the stylistic imperatives and moral absolutes of Dr Johnson and the Augustan period of the mid-eighteenth century, the only certainties in a frighteningly revolutionary age when so much else was in a state of flux or dispute.

Literary career

The three manuscript volumes of **juvenilia**, written between 1787 and 1793, were technically competent but heartless compositions. *Love and Freindship* (sic), written when she was 15, is probably the best-known juvenilia title, dedicated to her elder cousin Eliza. She wrote 'The History of England by a partial, prejudiced & ignorant Historian' when almost 16, humorously warning the potential reader that: 'N.B. There will be very few Dates in this History.' She adopted a mock heroic style to denounce and 'abuse' Elizabeth, to eulogise and 'prove the innocence of the Queen of Scotland' (Elizabeth's cousin, Mary Queen of Scots), and to express herself 'partial to the roman catholic religion'.

Although she had been writing since the age of 12, Austen's first published work came at the age of 35, and only four of her novels were published in her lifetime — *Sense and Sensibility* (1811), *Pride and Prejudice* (1813), *Mansfield Park* (1814), and *Emma* (1816) — and her name appeared on none of them. *Northanger Abbey* and *Persuasion* were published **posthumously** in 1818. *Pride and Prejudice*, completed in August 1797 when she was only 21, and before *Sense and Sensibility*, was offered to a publisher by Mr Austen on 1 November of that year, and promptly declined. In 1803 *Northanger Abbey* was sold to a publisher for £10, arranged by Henry, but Crosby did nothing with it. *Lady Susan* was a short novel in letter form, written in 1803, with a cynical **tone** and predatory female main character that seem to owe a lot to *Les Liaisons Dangereuses* (1782). Austen never tried to get it published, and after this exercise in feminine sexual wiles and wickedness she turned to less controversial and more ladylike material. This was followed by the unfinished novel *The Watsons* (the editorial title and not Austen's). When *Sense and Sensibility* was published in 1811 by Egerton it was on condition that she sustained any loss; it sold out in 20 months and made £140 for the author, as a result of which he bought *Pride and Prejudice* in 1812 and published it the following year. In November 1815 she was staying with Henry in London to see *Emma* through the printers. Now celebrated and admired by the Prince Regent, she dedicated this novel to him, at his request. Thereafter she began *Sanditon*, but died before finishing it.

Austen wrote two sets of three novels, with ten years between the sets. The first is distinctively eighteenth century and the second recognisably Romantic and therefore more modern in feeling. The last novel to be written, *Persuasion*, shows a new melancholy, sensitivity to seasons and nature, especially autumn, and use of pathetic fallacy. In the later works there is also comparatively less humour and dialogue, and more pathos, passion, reflection, secrecy and silence — though just as much vicious **satire**. There is a focus later on loss of love, which suggests that future works may have continued in an increasingly biographical as well as subdued vein. The unfinished novel *Sanditon* (originally called *The Brothers*), which was begun a few months before Austen's death and not published until 1925, takes her work in a new direction with its commercial seaside setting and range of social types. Her niece, Anna Austen Lefroy, attempted to complete it after it was willed to the latter by Cassandra on her death in 1845, but she only succeeded in producing a continuation.

Jane Austen's letters

Letters were most often written between female relatives, except for momentous occasions when men might correspond for practical purposes, as Mr Gardiner does from London to keep Mr Bennet informed of Lydia's situation. Sisterly or quasi-sisterly relationships are the most significant in all of Austen's novels, and letters served an important socially cohesive function in a large family whose members were often separated. Cassandra and Jane sent letters every three or four days when they were apart, and always had one on the go.

Readers of Austen's novels have sometimes been surprised and even shocked to discover the acerbity of the **wit** of her letters, which often mock an acquaintance in vitriolic and unfair ways, e.g. 'his legs are too short, and his tail too long'. Some biographers think she suffered from depression in Bath, and that these jibes are the result of an anger and bitterness towards her unmarried state, but this trait is already evident in her earliest writings, and she admitted to being a 'wild beast'. The full evidence of this side of her was not allowed to survive because Cassandra, aged 70, censored it by destroying all but 168 of her sister's letters, and all of those written before Austen was 20. Of those that survive, 95 are to Cassandra, who also burnt all of her own letters to her sister. Austen's more intimate letters to her sister were destroyed by Cassandra to protect Austen's reputation; she removed everything intimate about family or lovers, and thereby everything which could satisfy public curiosity about her sister, unfortunately leaving the impression that Austen was dedicated to trivia and gossip.

Even so the letters were considered quite shocking when first published in 1932, as not being consistent with expectation because of their perceived trivialities and occasional malice. They were criticised by Austen's great admirer E. M. Forster, and D. W. Harding described them as studies in 'regulated hatred'. They are mostly unparagraphed streams of consciousness that mix family matters with literary comments on her own and others' works. Her sense of **irony** and ridicule shine through clearly: she assassinates characters with waspish remarks and admits to being glad to have avoided meeting with them; there are tongue-in-cheek remarks such as 'I write only for fame, and without any view to pecuniary emolument' (14 January 1796 to Cassandra); there are **bathetic** ones such as 'I have read the Corsair, mended my petticoat, & have nothing else to do'.

Austen's early letters are certainly light and bright and sparkling, and show an affection for her family and a consciousness of everything going on in her little world, but not the wider one of politics and war, which she did not feel was appropriate for a woman to comment upon. Some of her comments reveal attitudes relevant to the novels, such as 'I am by no means convinced that we ought not all to be **Evangelicals**', which seems to be said without irony and explains the views on slavery and clerical duties expressed in *Mansfield Park*. Her letters do betray, however, what Marilyn Butler describes as a 'deepening seriousness of tone' as time passes, and what could be remorse for her 'flashes of malice'. It comes across that it irked her to be viewed as an impecunious spinster, even by branches of her own family.

There are also distinctive authorial features evident, such as the use of triple structures and extended complex sentences, but interestingly the remaining letters also contain many of the excesses of expression that she condemns in the speech habits of her characters: exclamation marks and dashes, intensifiers such as 'exceedingly', and even **hyperbole**: 'it is enough to kill one'. This evidence confirms the difference for Austen between reality and the moral world constructed for her novels, and the different expectations for private and public modes of address; the place for talk of food, clothing and other domestic trivia is in letters between sisters but not in the drawing room with visitors present.

Jane Austen's death

By the time Austen broke off from writing *Sanditon*, in March 1817, after 12 chapters, she was seriously ill of an unknown illness, possibly cancer. She went to lodge in College Street, Winchester two months later in order to be under the care of her doctor. She died in Cassandra's arms a few weeks afterwards, aged 41 and at the height of her powers. Though this was not considered a particularly young age to die at the time (and the Brontë family fared far worse), Austen's sister lived to be 70 and her brother the admiral reached the age of 91.

Austen's epitaph in Winchester Cathedral is here quoted in full:

> In memory of
> Jane Austen,
> youngest daughter of the late
> reverend George Austen,
> formerly rector of Steventon in this county,
> she departed this life on the 18th July 1817,
> aged 41 after a long illness supported with
> the patience and the hopes of a Christian.

The benevolence of her heart,
the sweetness of her temper, and
the extraordinary
endowments of her mind
obtained the regard of all who knew her and
the warmest love of her intimate connections.

Their grief is in proportion to their affection
they know their loss to be irreparable
but in their deepest affliction they are consoled
by a firm though humble hope that her charity,
devotion, faith and purity have rendered
her soul acceptable in the sight of her
REDEEMER.

Her obituary in the *Salisbury and Winchester Journal* reads: 'Her manners were gentle, her affections ardent, her candour was not to be surpassed, and she lived and died as became a humble Christian.' Cassandra wrote: 'She was the sun of my life, the gilder of every pleasure, the soother of every sorrow, I had not a thought concealed from her, & it is as if I had lost a part of myself.' Her brother Henry wrote a biographical note of a few pages in which he said that her life was 'not by any means a life of event'. In the 1940s the Jane Austen society was set up and a museum made of the cottage in Chawton in which she resided from 1809.

Pride and Prejudice

This was Austen's personal favourite of her works, which she referred to as her 'darling child' (letter to Cassandra, 29 January 1813), and it holds the accolade of being the most-read novel in the English language. Though *Emma* is generally regarded as her supreme technical achievement, for its handling of **narrative** mode and irony, many readers have a particular fondness for *Pride and Prejudice*. Austen said of its heroine: 'I must confess that I think [Elizabeth] as delightful a creature as ever appeared in print, and how I shall be able to tolerate those who do not like her at least I do not know.' This, her first mature novel, is shorter and more compressed than *Sense and Sensibility*, and more lively and humorous than later works, mainly because of the personality of its main character, who is the viewpoint wherever possible. The Bennet family is the largest of which she wrote, since she usually focused on a family of only two or three children. Sisters were important in her work, and having five at once gave her scope to explore this relationship. The relationship of Elizabeth with her sisters is the lifeblood of the novel, just as Austen herself was, as Edmund Wilson puts it (p. 39 *Jane Austen: Twentieth Century Views*) 'held suspended by the web of her original family ties'. In *Pride and Prejudice* all Elizabeth's sisters are a threat to her future in one way or another, and although their errors of judgement or character defects are turned into **comedy**, potential tragedy hovers throughout.

Pride and Prejudice was the first of the three novels so far to be unequivocally called a **romance**, *Sense and Sensibility* being more of a debate and *Northanger Abbey* more of a satire, as well as belonging partially to the **Gothic genre**. Though it has all the characteristics of romantic comedy — and indeed Shakespearean comedy, with its lively and faulty heroine, ironic presentation and humorous episodes, as well as its amusing minor characters — *Pride and Prejudice* appeals to those who would not normally read such a fiction genre, and has many male admirers. Austen's achievement in this novel was to combine wit, **drama** and the traditions of poetic satire with those of the sentimental novel. Like her other novels, it is also a *Bildungsroman*, in which maturity is arrived at only after a painfully humbling learning process.

Seventeen years is a long time between composition and publication (although *Sense and Sensibility* and *Northanger Abbey* fared no better, and the last was not even published in her lifetime). We know that she 'lop't and crop't' in her revision of her first draft of *Pride and Prejudice*; and some commentators believe she substantially revised the novel in 1811–12, as well as in 1802. There are some identifiable late additions that betray themselves by reference to recently published works, but otherwise we cannot know how the final version differed from the original, since no manuscript survives. Though it was first published, as usual for the time, in three volumes, it was posthumously squeezed into two in the third edition. It is known that she had disagreements with her publisher, who wanted her to make alterations to her love scenes in *Pride and Prejudice*. In 1811 she wrote to Thomas Egerton:

> You say the book is indecent. You say I am immodest. But Sir in the depiction of love, modesty is the fullness of truth; and decency frankness; and so I must also be frank with you, and ask that you remove my name from the title page in all future printings; 'A lady' will do well enough.

It is hard to imagine Austen being accused of indecency and immodesty; her reply is in the spirit and language of Elizabeth Bennet.

Regency England

Although there are no directly political references in *Pride and Prejudice*, the setting of the novel in her own historical period requires an understanding of the social and cultural milieu that provides the background to the causes of and reactions to the events of the **plot**. The period also marks the cusp between Classicism and **Romanticism**, so that elements of both can be found in Austen's work. The details of houses, forms of transport, and leisure activities play a significant role in creating environment and atmosphere, and often carry symbolism indicative of the character concerned; without an understanding of what was considered proper behaviour at the time one cannot share the creator's judgement of her characters.

Napoleonic Wars

England and France were at war throughout the period of Austen's writing, and her most famous novels were written and published during a time when there was a real danger of the French invading the country. The Napoleonic War was the largest-scale war on the European continent undertaken by England since the fifteenth century, and there was a clear political dimension: monarchical England was fighting against a revolutionary France that had executed its king, Louis XVI, in 1793 and replaced him with a revolutionary government led by Napoleon. There was widespread fear among the British upper classes of a popular uprising in Britain in sympathy. The American War of Independence and the French Revolution caused great strains in English political life; the loss of the American colonies was thought to be a great disaster, while the French Revolution was viewed as a real political threat, and one not averted until the decision to expand the electorate to include the urban working class in the Great Reform Act of 1832.

Austen was anti-Napoleon, being both anti-revolutionary by nature and the sister-in-law of a guillotine widow who later married her brother Henry. When *First Impressions* was written Napoleon was a general in the French army, but by the time *Pride and Prejudice* was published in 1813 he had become emperor of France and had tried to invade Russia. Critics have complained that one would not guess these momentous events from the novel; soldiers exist in it, but only as attractive uniforms to be viewed as potential husbands. The characters in all Austen's novels are, however, acutely aware of the political background — even if it does not impinge directly on their lives — as their speeches and opinions convey attitudes to security and change, tradition and class, rebellion and conformity, town and country.

The monarchy

George III, the third of the Hanoverian (German) kings of England, ascended the throne in 1760. Although he lived until 1820, he suffered from intermittent mental illness, and on several occasions Parliament transferred the monarch's powers to his son, the future George IV, who acted as Prince Regent. From 1810 onwards this arrangement became permanent, and this period, which came to be known as the Regency, coincided with a major upsurge in cultural life. The word 'Regency' came to be synonymous with elegance, refinement, style and taste. 'Beau' (George Bryan) Brummel (1778–1840) was at one time a personal friend and protegé of the Regent and the arbiter of taste and fashion in London, Bath and Brighton. Brummel established the mode of men wearing fitted, well-cut clothes adorned with an elaborately-knotted cravat, which was the prototype of the modern suit and tie but known at the time as 'dandyism'. He took five hours to dress, and recommended that boots be polished with champagne.

Much of the Prince Regent's social life was conducted in Brighton, where he had his famous pavilion built in 1815, after being confirmed on the throne in 1812.

Bath represents licentious behaviour in *Northanger Abbey*, and Brighton carries this stigma in *Pride and Prejudice*. It was dominated from 1783 to 1820 by the Prince Regent and his entourage, and it was also the site of one of the largest militia camps on the south coast. The Regent treated his wife, Princess Caroline, very badly, having returned to his long-term mistress, Mrs Fitzherbert, soon after his marriage. For this reason, and because of his notorious private life, extravagant lifestyle and addiction to fashion and gambling during times of war and hardship, he was disapproved of by many; Austen detested him and was therefore not best pleased to be asked by his librarian, Stanier Clarke, to dedicate *Emma* to him.

The beau monde

The London Season was a relatively short period of time beginning shortly after Easter, when Parliament opened, and ending on 12 August, when Parliament went into recess and the grouse-shooting season opened. Remaining in London once the Season was over was a serious social faux pas and no members of society were willing to be seen in town once all their acquaintances had gone to either their country houses or to seaside spas; the latter gave people of all ages a chance to enjoy fresh air, good company and good food. Visits to such resorts were essential for socially active and ambitious people, as these watering places were the hub of social life in the summer. The peak of the season, when the aristocracy and upper gentry attended, was the fortnight in June between the horse-racing at Derby and Ascot. At places such as Brighton, Weymouth and Bath, the inland spa, balls and assemblies much like those in London took place every night, while the days were filled with the social activities unique to resort life: garden, water, card and dancing parties, as well as attendance at the pump rooms, which were the venue for finding husbands, so that under the disguise of seeking the curative spa waters matrons could dispose of their daughters. Here, although still regulated by the conventions of Regency propriety, couples had opportunities to meet and get to know one another.

Political parties

Although England was described as having a constitutional monarchy, the king was sovereign only in name, real political power residing — as it still does — with the elected Parliament. England was the first country in modern Europe to enjoy a form of democracy, but it took most of the eighteenth century for its politicians to create a system which worked. During the century, two significant factions formed within Parliament, and they came to be known as the Whigs and the Tories. They are the distant ancestors of our present-day political parties: the Conservative Party is directly descended from the Tories, and the Liberal Democrats from the Whigs. (There was no organised party for Labour until the dawn of the twentieth century, because the vote was given to men only, and only those who owned property.)

The two political factions were originally divided more by social background than by policies. The Whigs were mostly urban merchants who believed in free trade and economic liberalism; the Tories tended to include the aristocracy, country landowners and the Church of England. Austen's father, being a minister with a country living, was inevitably a Tory supporter, and predictably the political leanings of his daughter's approved characters were Tory because of their belonging to the country gentry, always associated with conservatism. During the eighteenth century, the office of Prime Minister gradually came into being, but early Prime Ministers tended to be supported by shifting coalitions of factions rather than by clearly delineated parties.

Evangelicalism

A general term for earnest and personal Christianity, Evangelicalism embraced a range of new churches. Supporters of this movement, introduced in the mid-eighteenth century by John Wesley, the founder of Methodism, tended to be Whigs, since the movement arose in urban **contexts** and was opposed to the established church supported by the Tories and country dwellers. It was a home-grown reform movement in reaction to a perceived neglect by the established church of the rapidly expanding industrial towns and their inhabitants, and it created a faction within the existing ecclesiastical system.

Austen changed from being against the movement to being for it because it included a goal to reform morals and manners, emanating from the middle class upwards. She also became increasingly aware of and distressed by the apparent corruption and worldliness of the Church of England, as can be seen in her anti-clerical **characterisation** of Mr Collins and Mr Elton, both self-aggrandising and self-promoting smug social climbers with no genuine interest in serving their parishioners or setting a good moral example. Clergyman were not actually required to have a vocational calling (even Wickham intended to go into the church) or to do more than profess spiritual leanings; a preferment to a living, often in the gift of the local lord of the manor, was the offer of a means of subsistence with few duties involved, and even those could be delegated to a curate to allow for extended absences from the parish (Mr Collins is frequently away from home). The incumbent's political views and connections were generally held to be more important factors than their moral attitudes or aptitude for the pastoral role.

Society

The social hierarchy had not much changed since feudal times. The professionals, mainly doctors and lawyers, were considered upper middle class and were treated more kindly by the gentry than those whose money came from trade, since they were educated. There was a developing mutual hostility between town and country dwellers; the latter had traditionally enjoyed higher social status but increasingly could not compete with urban wealth, although they still retained land ownership. There was little love lost between the gentry and aristocracy, the latter being viewed by the former as proud, idle and undeserving; Lady Catherine de Bourgh in *Pride and Prejudice* is presented as a haughty bully. The truly worthy thing to be, in Austen's eyes, was a gentleman, hence Elizabeth's comment that she is a 'gentleman's daughter' even though her mother is not considered to be a gentlewoman because, although her sister married an attorney, her brother went into trade. It is a radical and provocative statement for Elizabeth to claim social equality with Darcy, whose mother, Lady Catherine's sister, was also titled, and whose grandfather was an earl.

The country gentry at this time were at the height of their influence and prestige; their ownership of land, and therefore effectively of the tenant farmers and agricultural labourers who went with it, gave unique autonomy to the English gentleman on his estate. (As late as the First World War they were still deciding which and how many of their employees to send off to war.) However, they recognised that they were under threat from the rise of an increasingly prosperous urban middle class who made their money from manufacturing. This social trend, accelerated by the industrial revolution, is represented by the Gardiners in *Pride and Prejudice*; they live in Cheapside, an unfashionable area of London, and are heartily despised by the Bingleys. This is ironic given that the Bingley fortune was all acquired through trade. Gradations of social standing were indicated by the size of one's property, by how many families one dined with, and by the type of carriage one owned (and to not have one at all, like Mrs Long, was a considerable minus point). That there was tension between town and country dwellers, and the former regarded themselves as superior, is shown in Caroline Bingley's criticism of Elizabeth for having 'an abominable sort of conceited independence, a most country town indifference to decorum' (p. 36).

Manners and morals

As far as etiquette was concerned, it was important at the time to be seen to do the right thing, and one would be gossiped about if one offended the traditions or broke the rules of the local and wider community. There were strict rules about visiting, and leaving one's card, and it is with just such a conversation that the novel begins. There were many pitfalls in the visiting game: it was a matter of courtesy for the head of the household to 'wait upon' a male newcomer to a neighbourhood, but it was a slight to visit before being visited, depending on the respective positions of those involved, or not to visit soon enough, or not to return a visit soon enough (and Jane is only finally convinced of Caroline Bingley's treachery when she is faulted in this matter). Furthermore, having 'called', one had to stay the right amount of time, which was 15 minutes, as both the maximum and minimum acceptable length of a

visit when calling on an acquaintance unannounced and uninvited. More or less would be interpreted accordingly, as it is in *Emma*. The caller had to leave a card if the 'callee' was not at home. One could not approach someone without being introduced, or introduce someone if one had not been previously and formally introduced oneself (making it a social faux pas of Mr Collins to introduce himself to Darcy in Chapter 18).

It was not until the nineteenth century that there was progression from a shame to a guilt culture, i.e. towards a private conscience whereby what the neighbours thought was less important than whether one could live with oneself. While Elizabeth suffers a degree of remorse for having been instrumental in allowing Lydia to run the risk of social stigma, she is also clear that Lydia's behaviour is unacceptable simply because of the shame it brings on the family, and this condemnation is shared by the author, who does not question the idea that living with a man out of wedlock ruins a girl. Elizabeth, the voice of reason and common sense at this point in the novel, condemns Lydia's behaviour as 'infamy' and declares that if Lydia does not marry Wickham 'she is lost forever'. The only voice of moral relativism belongs to Mrs Bennet, who is so happy to have Lydia married that she does not care about the manner of its accomplishment, whereas even Mr Bennet manages to condemn both his youngest daughter and Wickham, saying: 'I will not encourage the impudence of either, by receiving them at Longbourn.' Though she sometimes criticises sexism, Austen lets **bourgeois** morality alone.

Inheritance and prospects

Families with no sons, as is the case in the Bennet family, which has no direct male descendants, were to be pitied as property could not pass down to any of the girls but could be 'entailed' to the nearest male relative, in this case the reverend Mr Collins, a distant cousin of Mr Bennet who will inherit the family home of Longbourn on the latter's death. Only elder sons could inherit their father's estate (and his first name), and they were expected to involve themselves in politics as a way of ensuring the continuation of their family's privileges and interests. Alternative respectable occupations had to be found for younger sons: the second estate was the church, and the third was either the army or the navy (with the latter considered the 'senior service' as it was called the Royal Navy and was a national entity, whereas the army consisted of a collection of county regiments). Austen's brothers entered and rose through the ranks of the navy. The army, often 'redcoats' in literature as this made them more glamorous and dramatic, had a home barracks but were posted to small towns on recruiting drives; their pay was barely sufficient but their social status was quite high because the younger officers were eligible bachelors and therefore invited by the local gentry to all the balls and events in the vicinity.

It was an acquisitive society based on money and property, which could be acquired through marriage as well as inheritance. Dowries, allowances and being an heiress were prerequisites for women to be considered attractive marriage prospects, the monetary value of each of these determining their expectations. On the other hand, women were potentially more socially mobile than men, less categorised by their profession since they didn't have careers to be assessed. Provided they were gentlewomen or pretty, they could raise their social status through a good marriage (as Elizabeth and Jane do); it was more common for men than women to marry beneath them (and it is a disaster that Fanny's mother did so in *Mansfield Park*). The onus was on men to find someone rich to marry if they had no money themselves. To succeed in this objective they had to depend on charm or seduction, which could put young women's reputations in danger (as Wickham does three times — four including his flirtation with Elizabeth).

A woman's reputation (a **euphemism** for virtue or chastity) was vitally important to her whole family's social position as well as to her chances of attracting a suitor. When of age, which was 16, young females were paraded at balls to declare that they were 'out', so that eligible males could make their move. They were chaperoned by older married women, usually relatives, on the rare occasions they were allowed out in public. Except when dancing, it was almost impossible for single girls to have private conversations with men they were not at least engaged to, hence the excitement when a ball is announced, and the pressure Lydia puts upon Bingley to arrange one.

Courtship and marriage

Marriage was assumed to be the social and biological destiny for all women of all classes in the eighteenth and nineteenth centuries. As Byron said at around this time: 'Man's love is of man's life a thing apart, 'Tis woman's whole existence.' Austen explains the situation with reference to Charlotte Lucas: 'Without thinking highly either of men or of matrimony, marriage had always been her object; it was the only honourable provision for well-educated young women of small fortune, and however uncertain of giving happiness, must be their pleasantest preservative from want' (p. 120). This makes it clear how brave Elizabeth is being in turning down Mr Collins, for she cannot afford to be choosy. Austen herself turned down an offer she thought better of overnight, and became Aunt Jane as a result. Mary, being both plain and not at all accomplished, can expect to end up looking after her parents, pitied by society for being a spinster.

Marriage involved the wider family and not just the couple; Miss Bingley threatens Darcy with a 'charming mother-in-law' in the person of Mrs Bennet, and when Charlotte wins Mr Collins the whole family celebrates. The leading families looked to ally themselves with others of a similar rank, and often achieved this by the marriage of cousins so that the wealth and property could be kept in the family; this was Lady Catherine's plan for her daughter Anne and Darcy. Though wives were not independent in any sense, moving to their husband's establishment

was the only possible freedom girls could aim for, and it was therefore as devoutly wished for by them as by the parents, who would otherwise have to continue to support them. Independence required money, hence Emma's ability to claim that she will not marry. The only other (barely respectable) alternative was to become a governess, which offered a limited change of scene but a different form of servitude.

Matrimony being the final goal, everything leading to it or preventing it becomes a significant event: the balls and dance partnerships; the 'chance' encounters and returned visits; the setbacks and rivalries; the proposals and dowries. These topics and events took up all available time and dominated conversation among all females beyond puberty. Marriage was possible at 16 (the age of 'coming out', i.e. of making a debut at a ball to announce availability for suitors to make an offer to the father for the girl's hand in marriage); by 18 it was positively desirable, and by 20 the worries of being left on the shelf as an old maid began, hence Charlotte's (she is 27) determination to catch Mr Collins and his warning to Elizabeth (who is already 21).

Gretna Green was the nearest village over the Scottish border, and therefore not subject to English law, which took advantage of the laxer Scottish marriage laws during the 1754–1856 period to become a refuge for amorous couples who could have instant marriages with no questions asked. Since the Marriage Act of 1853 marriages in England could only be performed after a three-week period of residence and the declaration of banns, and with parental consent if under 21. It is assumed, and hoped, that Lydia and Wickham have eloped to Gretna Green, so that at least she is technically married rather than living in sin in London.

Although marriage itself was not considered a fit subject for novelists, and writers of this period (and for long after) allowed readers only incidental glimpses of what happened after the wedding, the lead-up to the great day provided a wealth of heart-searchings and plot twists, all based on the original romance model of the love triangle: two men desirous of marrying one woman, or vice versa. The comedy genre demands that all her heroines should find a partner, but some of Austen's views of marriage and comments on married couples she knows are very caustic in her letters, and not many marriages are held up for approval in her works. A meeting of intelligent minds, compatibility of views and equality of respect were the main ingredients for the successful recipe, although Mrs Gardiner tells Elizabeth that she knows the latter needs to look up to her husband 'as a superior'. Education was the cause and effect of Plato's 'intelligent love', which is why there is stress on the mutual benefits that Elizabeth and Darcy (and Emma and Knightley, Catherine and Henry, and Marianne and the Colonel) can offer each other: a reconciliation of youthful wit and mature wisdom, and a necessary containment of the dangerous individualism of the females within the established social order.

Titles

In Austen's work titles of address are an important mechanism for observing protocol and preserving propriety. As it was expected that girls in a family would marry in order of age, there was a convention that the eldest unmarried daughter in a family was called 'Miss' plus surname, hence Jane being referred to outside the family as 'Miss Bennet' and the other sisters by just their first name (and even by the author: 'Elizabeth was disgusted, and even Miss Bennet was shocked'). When socialising outside the family, where first names are not appropriate, the younger daughters are called by their full name, e.g. Miss Elizabeth Bennet (whereas Jane is never 'Miss Jane Bennet'). Spinsters of a certain age were also given the courtesy title 'Miss' without their first name, whether or not they had elder sisters (e.g. Miss Bates in *Emma*). Married woman immediately became known by their married title and husband's surname, and lost their first name, like Mrs Hurst. For girls to become 'Mrs' was a rite of passage much longed for, as in Lydia's case, since married women took precedence over older unmarried ones (as Lydia is quick to remind Jane when she visits home as Mrs Wickham).

Men were always referred to as 'Mr', hence the anomaly of the main characters in *Pride and Prejudice* being known as Elizabeth and Mr Darcy, not an equal partnership. (Many readers would not readily recall Bingley's, or even Darcy's, first names, so little are they used in the novel.) If the 'Mr' were dropped (and this was often considered impolite) it was the surname not the Christian name by which men were referred to. Even close friends observed distinctions of rank, did not use first names even in private, and especially not for a social superior; for example, the friendship in *Emma* is between Miss Woodhouse and Harriet, and Mrs Elton's calling Miss Fairfax 'Jane' and Mr Knightley just 'Knightley' are ways in which she reveals her vulgar manners. Family relationships required formal titles, so for instance Mrs Bennet refers to 'my sister Philips' and Elizabeth's letter from her aunt is signed 'M. Gardiner'. Married couples, and even when alone, referred to each other as Mr and Mrs plus their surname, as the Bennets do (and in fact they are not even given first names). Servants were usually called by their surname only, whether male or female.

Family life

The number of domestic servants was an indicator of status, and there were many ways in which they eased the life of the gentry, in addition to the obvious ones of providing and serving meals and doing the laundry and cleaning: fires needed constant attention; the silver had to be polished; water had to be heated and carried. They had a hierarchy of their own, housekeeper to scullery maid, with the lady's maid in a special category of her own as an intimate companion of the lady of the house. They spent long hours below stairs and slept in attics. Bonds with parents were not always strong at that time, when the children of gentry were brought up

by nurses and governesses and the father was often a physically or mentally distant figure, so that siblings often became very close, especially the females who had to stay at home so much. Lady Catherine is shocked that the Bennet girls did not have a governess (but nor did Jane Austen).

Though aristocratic couples kept separate bedrooms, the gentry did not, hence the large number of children conceived. Effective contraception was not available (only condoms made of animal gut), and often not practised at all. It was not unusual for a woman to be permanently pregnant, as was Elizabeth Austen, Edward's wife, until she died in or after one childbirth too many. The infant mortality rate was very high: 20% of babies died in their first year, and one in three children before their sixth birthday (the life expectancy was only 35 at the turn of the century) so that despite the number of children born, a large family was quite unusual. The aim of parents was to have sons (at least two, 'an heir and a spare'), so five daughters was considered a disaster, as each needed to be provided with a dowry or allowance to attract a husband. (It is fortunate for the human race that some daughters managed to be born before or between the sons.)

If they were unable to catch a husband (and they were considered to be 'on the shelf', like Anne Elliot in *Persuasion*, if they were still single by their mid-twenties) they were a lifelong financial burden to their nearest male relative, father then brother, and would live at home for the rest of their lives. In Austen's novels families with many children are often considered to be rather feckless and self-indulgent (despite the size of her own) and two is the ideal number she gives to the more socially elevated or approved of families: the Darcys, the Woodhouses, the Knightleys, the Tilneys.

Life revolved around letters exchanged between female family members, who were often apart because of extended visits to relatives for either the good of their own health or to attend to that of the relative. Letters were sent to the post office with a servant, or the local postman could be paid a penny to deliver them within the area; the 'penny post' was universally in operation then for local deliveries within a town or village. The transport between towns was by stagecoach, and charged according to distance and number of sheets. To save money, correspondents wrote very small and cross-ways between the lines. As well as being depended upon for information, letters were also considered a form of household entertainment to be read aloud at table for wider domestic consumption, and this had to be borne in mind when divulging intimacies. Lydia's typically unrestrained letters to Kitty are rendered unreadable, and therefore unable to be shared, by being 'too full of lines under the words'.

Daily life was lived very much in the public rooms of the house and privacy was hard to come by, and the desire for it disapproved of (as Mrs Norris disapproves of Fanny Price's 'spirit of secrecy, independence and nonsense'). 'Reflection must be reserved for solitary hours' (p. 206), which meant at night. Elizabeth frequently has to retire to her room to compose her agitated feelings and prepare to keep a secret from other members of the family; she 'hurried her away to her room' (p. 189) rather than face even her best friend Charlotte, because showing emotion in public was an even greater social crime. In addition to it being an offence against etiquette to withdraw oneself, there was a practical disincentive to withdrawing to one's room in that bedrooms were usually both unheated and shared with siblings. Men, however, had a library or study as a private place to escape to, and Mr Bennet makes a point of frequently doing so. Women took refuge in their ailments and took to their beds (Mrs Bennet) at a time when they were encouraged to fancy themselves nervous by medical works associating physical and emotional delicacy with gentility in the female sex.

Country life

Lords of the manor, apart from engaging in hunting, shooting and fishing, did very little, as they had stewards to see to the running of the estate, grooms to look after horses, stables and carriages, gamekeepers, gardeners and servants galore to do all the work required for the upkeep of house, garden and estate. When confined to the house the stereotypical master passed the time by gambling at cards, indulging in heavy eating, drinking quantities of claret and port and molesting the maid-servants. When changes in fashion for architecture or landscape demanded it, an expert would be brought in to redesign the house or garden, to add a wing or to cut down an avenue of trees (as discussed in *Mansfield Park*). It was not uncommon for large country properties to be rented out for a period of several months, as Netherfield Hall is, to town folk wanting to entertain grandly and to enjoy rural pursuits. The higher gentry usually had a house in London, as Darcy does, in addition to their country estate, so that they could be in town for the social season.

Travel was by horse-drawn carriage or on horseback (the latter only for men of low status or in an emergency), and slow. Horses could be hired, which were replaced at inns along the way, so that one could travel in one's own carriage but with 'post' horses, and this is how Lady Catherine goes to Hertfordshire from Kent. It took Elizabeth an overnight stop between Derbyshire and Hertfordshire and half of the next day to get home in a coach, arriving 'by dinner-time the next day'. The time taken by journeys was partly the reason why house guests stayed for a long time compared to the modern practice of a visit to friends or relatives; Lady Catherine tells Maria Lucas and Elizabeth that she expected them to stay two months, not a mere six weeks, at Hunsford. Being cut off from neighbours and towns, and with few diversions, country house owners encouraged visitors, especially those with an amusing talent, those who were famous or fashionable, or those who would make up a shooting party or ride to hounds. If not dancing, listening to singing or making polite conversation, visitors would be expected to join in card games, whist and quadrille being popular at the time. It must be remembered that without electricity and dependent on candles (which were expensive) even the wealthiest inhabitants

of country houses rose early and retired early to bed, and fitted activities requiring good vision, such as reading and sewing, into the hours of daylight.

The lady of the house, not having even sport as a hobby and largely confined to the house, passed her time when at home in embroidering, sketching, and piano-playing. Christmas was not yet a much-celebrated festival or family event (this happened later during the Victorian period) so the winter months were very quiet. She would expect to spend the social season in Bath or London, where she would attend plays and art exhibitions, the main aim being to be seen in public doing the latest things wearing the latest fashion, rather than to improve her education. Dancing was much prized by the young as a rare opportunity for men and women to converse privately and have some physical contact; it was condoned by parents as allowing legitimate proximity but not licentiousness. Unlike the sons, who were sent away to public schools at the age of seven, the daughters would be tutored at home, usually by a governess (Lady Catherine is shocked to discover that the Bennet girls did not have one) and were not expected to become proficient at anything more than domestic accomplishments and basic literacy and numeracy, their designated future role being to catch a husband, look after his house and entertain his guests (see Darcy and Elizabeth's discussion of a woman's education on p. 39). It was considered dangerous to over-educate a female child, as this would render them unmarriageable (Mary Bennet's fate).

Costume

What men and women wore had an effect, then as now, on the options and limitations of their behaviour. Full-length flimsy dresses — whose role was primarily decorative and intended for the drawing room — and elaborate hair styles restricted women's physical movements indoors and their ability to do much outdoors, such as go for vigorous country rambles, be out in inclement weather or ride horses seriously (when women did ride — and Elizabeth doesn't — they had to wear a long skirt and sit side-saddle for reasons of decorum and to be sure of remaining *virgo intacta*). They had no pockets or any way of secreting things about their person except into the cleavage of their empire-line frocks, a fashion brought in after the French Revolution to replace crinolines as a gesture of dissociation from the Bourbon dynasty. This was considered a wise move but these simpler gowns exposed the neck and made young ladies vulnerable to chills. Raincoats did not exist, nor cold-weather gear, and hats, gloves and footwear were decorative rather than functional. Though they had no umbrellas, parasols were *de rigueur* for ladies because a sun-tanned complexion denoted peasantry and having to work outdoors (Caroline Bingley scorns Elizabeth for having grown 'so brown and coarse').

Women possessed a limited number of 'gowns', as they were relatively expensive and had to be made to order by a seamstress, after material had been purchased from a local haberdasher, who often had to bring it from London. What to wear was an important and time-consuming matter for consideration, hence the flutter caused by an upcoming ball or any social engagement. The type and quality of the fabric, whether silk, linen, muslin or plain cotton, was an indication of social status. Re-trimming an old bonnet was often the only way of pretending to have a new one. Laundry was of course done by servants, under difficult circumstances in an English climate, and involved a whole day each week (Monday, when weekend guests had departed) of washing and drying, starching and ironing. Ladies who wore white were therefore considered more refined (see Elinor Tilney in *Northanger Abbey*) because of the implications for laundering it as well as because of its associations with purity. Hair was long, which required a maid to brush it in the evening, put it in papers overnight, and pin it up in the morning, often with the use of curling tongs, heated in the fire, for the fringe and side pieces.

Powdered wigs had disappeared by this time, but men's high collars made them stiff of head movement, and their cravats made them look formal at all times. Black was the favoured colour for coats, which were worn indoors and out, and not only for the clergy and doctors. It gave men a sober mien bordering on the sombre, which is why Wickham's blue coat stands out and is commented on, and the fascination of the 'red coats'.

Comedy and romance

Classical influence

Austen was influenced by the prose writers of the eighteenth-century Augustan period, such as Swift and Dr Johnson, who applied **classical** precepts to their writing genres and styles, and she allies herself with their conservative and rational world view by her adoption of social comedy as her main mode. The term 'classical' embraces nostalgia for and emulation of the literary practices and social values of Greek and Roman antiquity. These include a belief that only the intellect can raise us above an existence otherwise indistinguishable from that of animals, who live by their instincts and appetites. Elegance of expression and control of form are civilised virtues, and universal concerns are more enduring and important than those pertaining to the individual. As Dr Johnson said in *Rasselas*, it is the job of a writer to examine the species not the individual, 'to remark general properties and large appearance' rather than to 'number the streaks of the tulip'. The aim of classical writing is therefore usually **didactic** rather than affective, hence the tendency towards satire and **parody**, and the use of abstract nouns rather than specific **imagery**. Other features of style that Austen borrowed from the essayists, and which lend her work authority, are restraint and balance. Classical texts do not normally include references to animals, women, children or the lower classes, as the proper study of man is man as a political animal, and his role in the community and public

life. Their contexts, therefore, are usually urban and social, and dialogue, debate and rhetoric are dominant modes and devices.

Social comedy

Eighteenth-century literature favoured social comedy as a genre, as it was a vehicle for the satirising of institutions and **stereotypes** that they so enjoyed. The drama of the period had developed from the comedies of **humours** of Ben Jonson and other early seventeenth-century dramatists, in which a character who embodies a 'humour', e.g. melancholy, causes amusement when interacting with other character types. The Restoration plays at the end of the century picked up these characteristics when the theatres re-opened, and exaggeration and scurrilous wit continued to be the main feature of the eighteenth-century stage, with Richard Sheridan a famous provider of it. One feels that his works were never far from Austen's mind when she was creating dialogue for her silly and pretentious characters.

Austen wrote comic novels in the sense that they have resolutions and happy endings, in which the good are rewarded and the bad are punished, though not seriously and no one dies. They end with marriage, and in the case of *Pride and Prejudice* there is the conventional Shakespearean comedy ending of triple nuptials. They fall specifically into the genre of social comedy, sometimes called **comedy of manners**, which means they study public behaviour and relationships, and it is in relation to the characters' speech and actions to others that they judge each other and the reader judges them. The classical literary tradition (as opposed to the Romantic one which deals with solitude and introspection) is based on Plato's philosophy that man is only complete when a member of society, which enables him to compare himself to others and learn from this how to perfect himself.

Comedy of manners

Austen's form of social comedy is that which mocks the attitudes and behaviour of particular social groups, usually those that consider themselves fashionable and superior. Comedies of manners are necessarily set in interiors; drawing rooms where people meet, mix and reveal their dubious morals and affectations. It is a didactic genre, because vice and virtue are debated and characters are appropriately punished or rewarded, as well as an entertaining one dependent on intelligence, wit and nuance of language. Though there may be liaisons effected and marriages arranged, they are less of the heart than of the head, with little romance — in the modern sense — involved. Money and property are of paramount importance in social comedy, and expediency a driving force; to put it at its lowest, the world depicted by Austen is a market place dedicated to 'selling teenage virginity for cash and crenellations' (A. A. Gill, *Sunday Times Culture*, 6 January 2008). *Les Liaisons Dangereuses* (1782) is a good example of the cynicism involved in the promises given and broken, the matches made and unmade, in a comedy of manners.

Austen's works conform to Horace Walpole's dictum: 'This world is a comedy to those that think, a tragedy to those that feel.' She encourages thinking rather than feeling, and therefore, like Chaucer, another observer of social mores, she is able to perceive the ludicrous and therefore the targets for satire, which are often those who claim to have feeling (like Mrs Bennet who suffers from her 'poor nerves' and has to retire to bed when anything upsetting happens) and who do no thinking at all. For Austen sense was more important than sensibility, and more necessary for a healthy individual life and a robust social system, in which sound choices are based on knowledge and judgement.

Her aim is not to pander to the needs of the individual, and even less to preach the overturn of society, but only to make it possible for someone perceptive and sensitive to be able to reconcile themselves to their relationships and place in the social context, flawed though this is. Feelings of a deep and private nature are not expressed by the characters of her novels; even when struck by embarrassment and remorse, her heroines are most concerned about justice, propriety, decorum and other social virtues, and how they will be perceived by others, rather than about how they will survive their personal anguish. We are told as a matter of fact that Elizabeth thinks she has lost Darcy and Pemberley, but we do not experience her suffering. It was not considered decorous to expose one's private trauma, since it would discomfit others, and in any case fortitude is a Christian virtue. How different from the next generation of female writers, such as the Brontës, who revealed their own emotions in their writing and allowed their heroines — think of Cathy in *Wuthering Heights* — to do the same, and to an extraordinary degree. This is not to say that Austen's heroines, including Elizabeth, do not show evidence of incipient Romanticism, but it takes the form of independence of spirit rather than depth of passion.

Romance

The genre of romance can be defined as pertaining to adventure, heroic exploits, the winning of love and the facing of obstacles. Literature has utilised this formula since the medieval period, and still does; the idea of the course of true love not running smooth provided the basis for Arthurian legends, Shakespeare comedy and much modern fiction in book and film form. It can be turned to both comedy and tragedy, depending on whether the lovers are separated (by death or imprisonment) or united at the end. The prerequisite for either is that the lovers should be idealised or exceptional, that the misunderstandings should be serious, that the opposition should be threatening, that chance, irony and fate should play significant parts, and that the future happiness or misery of the couple should be indisputable. These criteria can all be successfully applied to *Pride and Prejudice*, which gets closest to being tragic at the point when Elizabeth realises what she has thrown away and thinks it is too late; but then comedy appears in its smiling mask in the unlikely form of Lady Catherine, who by attempting to ensure a tragic outcome actually brings about a comic resolution, typical in its multiple marriages and trouncing or humbling of the enemies. Darcy's performance as combatant against his evil enemy, Wickham, and his success as the modest and unsung saviour of her sister in order to please his mistress, makes him a quintessential romantic hero.

Romantic comedy novels traditionally stop just before or just after the wedding ceremony, and often with the fairy-tale ending of a betrothal and the promise of happy ever after. We do not know what transpires later in the relationship and do not witness its transformation to mundanity and disillusionment. We can see, however, that something went badly wrong with the Bennets' marriage, and their function is as a warning to Elizabeth and to the reader of the importance of judging by temperament and intelligence rather than, or at least as well as, physical attraction when choosing a partner for life.

Romanticism

The term Romantic, not actually coined until 1860, refers to the period of art, music and literature that falls roughly between 1775 and 1825. This period had a very different social and cultural focus from the preceding Augustan one of Dr Johnson et al. Though Austen deals with social issues, she also looks at the causes and effects of behaviour arising from individual personality, which makes her proto-Romantic in that the plot derives as much from their choices and behaviour as it does from social imperatives. The proof of this is that no two of her characters are alike, and many of them are complex and cannot be easily pigeon-holed into one category. By including women as main characters to be reckoned with — and who are not simply harridans, victims or *femme fatales* — Austen reversed the Augustan practice of either ignoring or stereotyping women.

Romanticism's chief tenets were the importance of childhood, passion, the personal, love and Nature. According to this approach to life, feelings are to be trusted rather than thoughts, and impulses followed are better than rules obeyed. Romantics champion rebellion, non-conformity and the cause of the lone individual against the system. They prefer to be outdoors and revere Nature as a divine force, believing that those who cut themselves off from their natural roots in the countryside will perish spiritually. Because of the inevitability of loss, pain, physical decay and old age — unless pre-empted by an early death — the Romantic mode is essentially a tragic one. The love triangle is the staple of many Romantic plots, with the wrong choice of partner leading to disaster and death.

In comedy, however, a first wrong choice can be rectified as it is in Austen's novels, and her sympathies for Romantic characters and philosophies is, to say the least, limited: the traits of whimsy, affectation, egotism and self-indulgence are satirised (for instance in Isabella Thorpe in *Northanger Abbey* and Marianne Dashwood in *Sense and Sensibility*), and rebellious or radical traits are presented as dangerous to the community and to society as a whole (as illustrated by Mr Yates in *Mansfield Park* and Frank Churchill in *Emma*). Elizabeth's breaking of convention and etiquette in going on foot through mud to Netherfield can only be condoned because of her concern for her sick sister and need to take on the parenting role because of the negligence of her mother, and we are given licence to support Elizabeth in her dirty petticoat only because it is the unpleasant and jealous Miss Bingley who criticises her for it. Elizabeth also plays the Romantic heroine in being adamant that she will marry only for love; nonetheless, she must learn to moderate her liveliness with silence, and to curb her Romantic tendencies of secrecy, imagination, impulse and hasty judgement by the end of the novel. As one would expect, Austen's admired characters avoid extremes and display a balance of sense and sensibility in accordance with Aristotle's recipe of the **golden mean**. However, they are Romantic in that they appreciate the countryside and dislike the town, and it is always in an urban context that unhappiness and decadent behaviour originate, as illustrated by Jane's trip to London and Lydia's to Brighton.

Romantic heroes and heroines

Despite spanning many centuries, the youthful Romantic hero and heroine, derived from medieval court life, have changed very little, even in outward appearance. Heroes have an exotic or aristocratic name and are tall, dark, handsome, sensitive, moody, athletic and bold. They are horsemen and/ or swordsmen, or the equivalent, as well as intelligent (Darcy is a great reader). Their job is to save their country, friends and helpless females through brave and selfless exploits. Heroines have polysyllabic names, are attractive with long dark hair and fiery eyes, and behave unconventionally, proudly, wilfully, and secretively. They are dependent, long-suffering and misunderstood, often because they were born into the wrong family and are virtually orphans. They provoke envy in other women, desire in men, and await deliverance — in the form of being rescued and carried off by the equivalent of a knight in shining armour. Elizabeth Bennet is close to a traditional Romantic heroine, and Darcy has most of the attributes of a fairy-tale prince. The dividing line between Romantic hero and villain, and Romantic heroine and *femme fatale*, is a narrow one, and only 'by their works ye shall know them'. Elizabeth, like so many literary heroines before her, initially mistakes one for the other and confuses Wickham with Darcy, the false with the true.

The rise of the novel

Novels, as their name suggests, were a comparatively late literary invention; the only prose that existed before the seventeenth century was in the form of sermons and improving moral tales, such as Bunyan's *The Pilgrim's Progress*. Prose, unlike drama and poetry, was not considered an appropriate medium for entertainment. A novel (or novella if relatively short) is defined as a fictional prose narrative having a plot unfolded through the actions, speech and thoughts of its characters. Its origin is commonly associated with Daniel Defoe, who wrote the first person prose fictions *Moll Flanders* and *Robinson Crusoe* at the beginning of the eighteenth century.

By the end of the Augustan period, three-volume satirical, confessional and **picaresque** novels were well established, and romantic novels were appearing in response to an increased educated, middle-class, female readership, house-bound and in need of diversion, catered for by the invention of circulating lending libraries. Once there was a market to be satisfied, writers began to produce novels, and very long ones, since they were serialised and therefore paid by the word. Until the nineteenth century they were usually comic rather than tragic — the former being more palatable to the taste of the time — and often had a fashionable Gothic element, one associated with romance since the Middle Ages. Austen's *Northanger Abbey*, begun in 1798, was inspired by the Gothic novels of Anne Radcliffe (1764–1823), though Austen subverted the genre by satirising it as well as making use of its conventions in order to make a moral point. For the first time female authors were now being published, other notable names being Fanny Burney (1752–1840) and Maria Edgeworth (1767–1849).

At around this time journalism also came into being, and was used to comment on social topics and attack individuals in positions of power or the public eye through the new media of newspapers, journals and pamphlets. Topical and subversive ballad **broadsheets** were a stage in the development of comic novels that included satire.

Epistolary novels

There was a vogue for **epistolary** novels in the eighteenth century that is still apparent in the works of Austen. *Sense and Sensibility* was originally entirely in letters and called *Elinor and Marianne*, as was *First Impressions*, the earlier version of *Pride and Prejudice*. The novel still contains references to 44 letters, and without their existence the plot could not function (see pp. 86–87). They enable those in different places for extended periods to communicate regularly and, if necessary, immediately. Letters are particularly important in Chapters 48 and 49 when Lydia is being sought in London by Mr Gardiner and Mr Bennet, who need to report the developing situation to Longbourn. The tension builds up as the letters are anxiously awaited and delayed and the reader knows no more than the Bennet family.

Their other function is to enable characters to reveal secrets and also convey their attitudes and personalities; sometimes they confirm what we already know about the letter-writer, as in the case of Mr Collins and Miss Bingley, but with the more complex characters letters can be a revelation, as in Darcy's case. They are as good as or better than the speaking voice for providing evidence of their writers' command of language and manners, as they are an extended utterance that allows the recipient and the reader to form a considered judgement based on extensive evidence. It is actually a moral imperative in Austen's works for an approved character to be able to write a letter, as indicated by Emma's being willing to allow that Robert Martin, the farmer, writes like a gentleman, and in his case it is all we get to hear of his voice.

The epistolary mode is easily parodied for its lack of realism because writing to the moment, and in the present tense, seems an unlikely activity when the writer is being or has just been either physically or mentally traumatised. This, in addition to its predictability and lack of variety, was presumably a reason why the genre had become unpopular and was dying out when Austen was writing. Until her time epistolary novels were melodramatic and contained scenes of rape or seduction, i.e. they had a sexual content, but she used letters only as a literary device in the interests of plot or character development, or to make a moral point, which was less of a lure for the prurient reader.

Epistolary novels concerned the romantic pursuit of gentry women by their aristocratic social superiors, e.g. *Pamela*, or *Virtue Rewarded*, a novel by Richardson published in 1740. Austen was an admirer of Richardson and adapted one of his novels as a play to be performed by the Austen family. However, epistolary novels are liable to misinterpretation by the reader since the author cannot directly steer them towards the required response; the character often exerts a fascination unintended and undesirable, even when they are a rapist, as in Richardson's *Clarissa*, and we can see this rehabilitating effect in the letter from Darcy. Even villains can sound attractive in letters, and are liable to be taken at face value without a mediating voice. Austen decided she preferred to embed her correspondence between characters in a narrative that has an ironic voice to remind us to read with discernment and even suspicion.

Realism

One of the most radical features of the new genre of the novel was its attention to domestic and other detail, since their aim was to convince the reader of the specificity of the environment and the individual, whereas previously allegorical prose works deliberately wanted the context to be a very general one, vague as to place and time and therefore universal as to application. Realism as a term and movement surfaced in the mid-nineteenth century, but it is relevant to consider to what extent Austen was trying to write realistic novels. Insofar as she attempted to describe human behaviour and surroundings, and to represent figures and objects exactly as they act or appear in life, to dwell on particularity, and to present the truth of individual experience, she can be said to adhere much more to realism than did her predecessors Sterne, Fielding or the female Gothic novelists. There is also a consciousness of duration of time and space (dates and places are very specific in *Pride and Prejudice*) and of the need for convincing dialogue that show that she was aiming for veracity.

However, where she is still following previous tradition is in the employment of traditional plots, in the avoidance of the description of passionate or unsavoury scenes, and in the unwillingness to enter deeply and unselectively into the personality of the character. Austen uses less physical detail of appearance than most of her contemporaries, and much less description of decor and furniture and buildings, inside and out, and with little mention of food. This has the effect of focusing the reader's attention on the abstract rather than the concrete, in the traditional didactic way; she actually mocks those of her characters who are only interested in domestic trivia and clothing, and the more vague the appearance of her heroine, the more the reader can identify with her, so we get very little by way of description of Elizabeth other than her sparkling eyes.

The three-volume novel

The reason the three-volume novel predominated from the early years of the nineteenth century was that the only way a publisher could expect to make a decent profit on books that appealed to a minority of people who had the taste, education, and money for middle-class fare was to sell the text in three separate parts. Charles Mudie's circulating lending libraries created a reader expectation of three volumes of about 270 pages each, to be rented by the volume. *Pride and Prejudice* went through two editions as a three-volume novel, in the same year, but became two volumes for the third edition in the year of Austen's death, 1817.

This lengthy format affected all aspects of the content and structure of the late eighteenth- and nineteenth-century novel: copious dialogue, events and characters; many chapters; complex plot lines; and **climax** points at the end of each of the first two volumes.

Austen and feminism

Contemporary women writers

The rise of women writers — though there were only a handful of them — coincided with the rise of the novel, which was, thanks to eighteenth-century circulating libraries, catering for bored and closeted females interested in the escapist fantasy literature of romance and Gothic horror. Women wrote letters every day (it was one of their morning duties, along with menu planning and making brief calls on their neighbours), so for them the epistolary novel was a natural extension of this social chore which was also a diversion. Early female novelists often used their writing to gain the attention and approval of their fathers, as Charlotte Brontë and Austen herself did, and Elizabeth Bennet seems to wish to please her father by her use of words and wit.

Austen felt compelled by social disapproval of women writers to describe herself as merely, but categorically, 'A Lady' on the title page of *Sense and Sensibility*; this need to conceal female identity continued throughout the nineteenth century, with the adoption of male pseudonyms by the Brontë sisters (Acton, Ellis and Currer Bell) and by Mary Ann Evans as George Eliot. (The need for protective deception or the financial expediency of adopting a first name or initial suggestive of masculinity was still being practised by U. A. Fanthorpe, Stevie Smith and A. S. Byatt in the late twentieth century). Publishers usually turned down would-be lady novelists by return, or allowed their manuscripts to languish unpublished for years even after being accepted for publication, as happened with *Pride and Prejudice* and *Northanger Abbey* respectively. Throughout the following century and beyond, women's writing was presumed to belong to, or was associated with, the 'lesser' genres of children's books, letters, diaries, cookery books and other domestic works, which were the only readily available, and very narrow ('two inches of ivory'), channels through which women could bring to light the private lives of one half of humanity.

Early female writers found it incompatible to be wives and mothers as well as writers, and did not attempt both. In 1928 Virginia Woolf laments that without a room of one's own, a luxury women did not traditionally possess, they could not become creative artists. Sylvia Plath, as late as the mid-twentieth century, despaired of being able to fulfil her roles as both mother and poet. Men, whether writers or not, usually had a study or library to retreat to (as illustrated by Mr Bennet). Because they had no privacy, no domestic 'time-out', and often no family or social support or encouragement for their talent or ambition, women writers had an uphill struggle, even when they had neither husband nor children to look after. Austen had to write covertly in the public parlour. Virginia Woolf tells us 'She was always interrupted…Jane Austen wrote like that to the end of her days', and she quotes James Edward Austen-Leigh's memoir, which says that his aunt 'was glad that a hinge creaked, so that she might hide her manuscript before any one came in'. Austen was very much at the mercy of the dictates of her male relatives and dependent on them for a roof over her head to the end of her life, which limited her freedom to satirise or openly condemn male pursuits and sources of income of which she disapproved, such as hunting and slavery.

Silence and submission

Though the word and concept 'proto-feminist' did not exist, some writers are before their time; the argument for Austen as a proto-feminist rests on how unconventional Elizabeth Bennet and her other heroines can be proved to be, on the degree of their independence of mind, and on their role as a catalyst for change. Those who do not accept that Austen was a feminist cite the marriages with which the novel ends, which they see as confirming the patriarchal traditions and social expectations of a

woman gratefully agreeing to settle down with an older, richer and more experi-enced man, and thereby entering into an unequal partnership. Elizabeth, as mistress of Pemberley, could have continued to be a thorn in the flesh of the nobility and establishment with her cutting observations, but the novel specifically tells us that she has learned to suppress her critical and teasing tendencies, and has even accepted the presence of Lady Catherine de Bourgh in her house. Although Mr Collins is mocked for his view that rank inevitably excites 'silence and respect' (p. 104), it could be argued that these are exactly the qualities that Elizabeth is forced to embrace as the price of her alliance with the Darcy clan. Tony Tanner (Penguin appendix) says: 'In the figure of Elizabeth Bennet [Austen] shows us energy attempting to find a valid mode of existence within society.' Though she is not impressed by the 'stateliness of money and rank', rather the reverse, she has to accept its power in the end; her 'wit and vivacity' are finally tempered with 'silence and respect', as recommended by Mr Collins.

Historically and in literature women were the silent gender, at best the listeners not the talkers, and often not even in a position to listen, as their role was in the private not the public sphere, and without influence. Elizabeth, like Shakespeare's Katerina in *The Taming of the Shrew*, has to be taught to keep her sharp tongue under control out of deference to the patriarchal system and in the interests of social and domestic harmony, and Mrs Bennet is satirised for not doing so. However much Austen may resent having to gag her heroine, the social reality was that they had to learn to be subservient, which means not speaking unless spoken to, and then in a voice 'soft, Gentle, and low, an excellent thing in woman' (*King Lear*). Their eyes were likewise meant to be modestly downcast, which is why much is made of Elizabeth's frank, observant and lively gaze. As in Shakespeare's *The Taming of the Shrew* the conventions of the genre of comedy, as well as the demands of social harmony, require the female with the sharp tongue to control it and defer to her lord and master. In the Middle Ages nagging or critical women were ducked in the village pond to teach them to know their place through a physical punishment; in Austen's works they are taught a moral lesson of humiliation through making a false judgement that has embarrassing consequences. Though spirited at first, and a supporter of love marriages, and willing to take the risk of turning down the odious Mr Collins, Elizabeth conforms at the end to the feminine ideal of the helpmeet who will teach her husband to become a better person and do her duty as a good wife, and mistress of the house. The earlier Elizabeth is a female artist figure, ima-ginative, articulate, in control of her life and able to use barbed words as a weapon to defend herself from banality and being imposed upon or beholden; she lays down her weapon, however, after winning her duel with Lady Catherine.

In tragedy, unconventional women are punished for being different, and therefore potentially dangerously subversive, by being killed by their author according to the evolutionary principle that they are not fit to survive and society has rejected them. They often die by fire or water (nature's retribution for unnatural behaviour), or their wicked double does on their behalf, as in *Jane Eyre*. In comedies difficult women are allowed to marry as an alternative, but only after they have tamed themselves or been tamed, have quelled their passions and rebellious spirit, and have accepted their place quietly in society. Elizabeth has learnt to keep her thoughts and words to herself by the end; she holds back with Darcy, telling herself that 'he had yet to learn to be laught at, and it was rather too early to begin' (p. 351). She has paid for her daring: 'She was humbled, she was grieved; she repented, though she hardly knew of what' (p. 295). The 'what' is simply being a female who dares speak.

Austen defers to the economic, social and political power of men, and draws attention to how female survival depends on winning male approval and protection; the happy ending is always that the heroine finds a better father in her husband. Though Austen would probably have supported the sentiment expressed by the heroine of *Sir Charles Grandison*: 'Is not marriage the highest state of friendship that mortals can know?' (quoted in Tomalin p. 71), she does not manage to establish that friendship as an equal one in her novels, since the social system and its gender relations could not support such a fantastical notion.

Resistance and escape

The alternative viewpoint, that Austen was indeed a feminist, is put by Gilbert and Gubar (1979) in *The Madwoman in the Attic*, their seminal work on the woman writer and the nineteenth-century imagination. Vivien Jones (introduction to Penguin classics edition of *Pride and Prejudice*) also claims feminist credentials for Austen's heroine: 'Elizabeth Bennet seems to connect most directly with the active, visible, independent identity of modern femininity', and she sees her as stronger than Darcy in that 'his social and moral confidence are challenged by her uncompromising criticism'. Apologists for Austen argue that the personal is political and that the debates going on in the novel reflect those of society at large, which was going through a period of turmoil and conflict between revolutionary (such as Mary Wollstonecraft in her *Vindication of the Rights of Woman*, 1792) and traditional values (such as Hannah More), a clash of values that particularly impacted upon attitudes to women and class. The former camp complained that women had no scheme to sharpen their faculties or focus their energies other than how to get married, and that their only route to self-improvement was through marrying well, whereas More's *Strictures on the Modern System of Female Education* (1799) give the following as guidance for young women (quoted on page xxiii of intro): 'Girls should be led to distrust their own judgment [...] they should be accustomed to expect and to endure opposition [...] they should early acquire a submissive temper and a forbearing spirit.'

These opposing views cover the decade during which *First Impressions* became *Pride and Prejudice*. In the context of More, Elizabeth stands out even more

prominently as a young woman who has no intention of following the prescription of restraint and submission for the achievement of happiness. Charlotte Lucas is one who has followed it, but the outcome is not seen to be happiness of a very high order. Elizabeth's appeal to Collins to treat her as a 'rational creature' is a direct echo of Wollstonecraft's demand that women be allowed to break the traditional codes of femininity, which were that they should be elegant, decorative, vulnerable, in need of protection and generally lady-like. Whereas Collins is the old-style would-be knight condescending to rescue a damsel he perceives to be in distress, Darcy is the new type of saviour who admits to being in need of salvation himself, and who treats Elizabeth as an independent being and an intellectual and spiritual equal.

Writing about their unsatisfactory lives was therapeutic for intelligent, imaginative women, and probably kept many of them sane, as it does for long-term prisoners of many kinds. Ironically, the very act of wanting to write was considered evidence of or a cause of insanity. *The Yellow Wallpaper* by Charlotte Perkins Gilman is a classic nineteenth-century text for conveying the paternalism of husbands and doctors and the lack of understanding of women's physical and mental states. In this long short story the wife is suffering from post-natal depression, which is diagnosed as mental illness, the prescribed remedy for which is the confiscation of reading matter and writing equipment. This, of course, makes her more frustrated and disturbed than before, and she starts to have hallucinations, thus seeming to confirm that she is indeed mad, rather than just creative and imaginative.

Many commentators have noted the obsessive imagery of confinement in women's writing of this period and later. Women were literally imprisoned in men's houses (symbolising chastity) — first their father's then their husband's — and also metaphorically constrained by boredom, chaperones, waiting for proposals, the iron bands of codes of conduct and the threat of losing their 'reputation' if they disobeyed. When Harriet Smith dares to walk alone in *Emma* she is symbolically attacked by gypsies. Much of their writing concerns, unsurprisingly, actual escape and imagery of escape. Elizabeth falls in love with the spaciousness of Pemberley. Although we are invited to condemn Lydia's elopement, we are not unsympathetic to her need to escape her father's house and the tedious company of her mother and younger sisters; though we must condemn those who are motivated by a 'hatred of home, restraint, and tranquillity' (*Mansfield Park*), we can understand why they feel so, and the need Elizabeth has to get away from the enclosure and claustrophobia of the family parlour and to break some rules, which she does by dirtying her petticoat in walking two miles in the mud.

Patriarchal attitudes

Feminists like Gilbert and Gubar see Austen as a critic of patriarchy and sexual exploitation, especially in the juvenilia, because she exposes the desperate need to catch a man and how it makes young women vain, manipulative and deceitful; Lydia is living out the plot and role of a heroine of popular romantic fiction. They argue that Austen is pointing out that such literature legitimises the role of men as rapist seducers, and that 'men have had every advantage of us in telling their own story', as Anne Elliot, the most feminist of Austen's women, points out.

Western literary genres are essentially male, devised by male authors to tell male stories from a male perspective. Heroes, travellers, overreachers, money-makers, performers, rakes, detectives, criminals, adventurers: these are all patterns of maleness in a patriarchal system. In addition, publishers, magazine editors and critics were also male, so a would-be woman writer who did not actually want to pretend to be a man was trapped into choosing one of two invidious alternatives: excusing herself as 'only a woman' or claiming to be 'as good as a man', i.e. to be either self-deprecating or unnatural, both suffocating and psychologically destructive positions for them to adopt. Thus the self-respecting female writer appeared to conform to patriarchal literary standards while actually subverting them, and the reader must look below the surface for obscured meanings and hidden revolutionary impulses.

It has been argued that Austen is being subversive in that while simultaneously appearing to punish assertive female behaviour and to recommend restraint and docility, she duplicitously reveals the delights of non-conformity and rewards her heroines for their rebellious traits; this comes through strongly in both the Collins and Lady Catherine put-down scenes, and in Elizabeth being awarded the ultimate prize of Darcy. In addition, many critics, not all feminists, have noted the lack of conviction of her endings, the way couples are brought with indecent authorial haste and apparent authorial indifference to the altar and the brink of a supposed wedded bliss.

Gilbert and Gubar also argue, though perhaps unconvincingly, that though she is a supremely unattractive character, Lady Catherine has independence and bows to no expectations but her own; she is a powerful and furious female who 'sees no occasion for entailing estates from the female lines' (p. 161) and is therefore opposed to the very basis of patriarchy, which is the exclusive right of male inheritance. She is vilified as a representative of matriarchal power because she is patronising, egotistical and rude, which is her 'cover' story, but to dig deeper one can see a proto-feminist who is surprisingly similar to Elizabeth in being forthright, authoritative and strong-willed. 'You give your opinion very decidedly for so young a person' (p. 162) could be a compliment rather than a criticism. When Elizabeth marries Darcy she takes the intended place of Lady Catherine's daughter, one much more in her own image than her real daughter, and it is thanks to her ladyship that the couple are brought together, though the primary reading is, of course, that Lady Catherine is endeavouring to keep them apart and is disgusted by the very notion of young women having opinions of any kind.

Unity and reconciliation

Vivien Jones argues that Elizabeth is a post-feminist rather than a pre-feminist heroine, who supports what is valuable from both the traditional and radical stand-points and is thus a force for change as well as reconciliation and consolidation. She claims that a resolution is achieved whereby the old and new are synthesised in the union of the mercantile money of the enterprising class of the Gardiners, with the old money and property of the ruling elite of the Darcy family. This union brings revolutionary tendencies into the fold where they can do no damage and where they can provide vitality and reinvigoration. This is prefigured by Darcy and Mr Gardiner combining forces to save Lydia's name and the Bennets's position in society.

So it can and has been argued that Austen is both advocating feminism yet not. Like all ironists she can utilise an idea while simultaneously exposing its fallacies: she ridicules polite conversation while utilising it; in *Northanger Abbey* she makes a plot twist out of Gothic imagination after mocking that very thing; she was not in favour of moralist writers, though is undoubtedly didactic herself; she attacks false literary conventions that debase expression and encourage female fantasies and dangerous delusions, but makes use of conventional romantic plots; she does deal with adultery, sexual attraction, intrigue and danger, but in an understated way which ensures that it gets overlooked; she parodies Fanny Burney in *Pride and Prejudice*, and all those whose fictions 'contribute to the enfeebling of women' (*The Madwoman in the Attic* p. 121), yet makes Elizabeth capitulate and join the arrogant, unfeeling and humourless social class she previously despised. Though she mocks patriarchal structures, Austen must inhabit them — as did Chaucer, a much earlier ironist. She can only make use of the materials from which they were built, and make a virtue of her own confinement, however suffocating; since her heroines were born female, they have no real choice in the matter or manner of their living. Austen's only personal act of defiance was to decide that if she could not be an Elizabeth Bennet, she would at least not become a Charlotte Lucas.

Critical history

Austen is no longer just an author; she is a cultural icon whose name is permanently inscribed on literature courses from GCSE to degree level. She has moved from being viewed as a insignificant entertainer to a serious moralist, and it is now better appreciated at a time when humour and ethics are not necessarily mutually exclusive. She has always tended to evoke the extremes of adoration or condescension, depending on the reader's political views — and still does in the twenty-first century — but generally the regard in which she is now held is higher than the way in which she was viewed by her contemporaries and the reputation she enjoyed during the nineteenth century. *Pride and Prejudice* remains one of the most

widely read novels in English and in 2005 was voted the most romantic novel of all time.

Austen's contemporaries

Sir Walter Scott's review of *Emma* in *Quarterly Review* in 1816 boosted Austen's reputation. He praised her delineation of minor characters, through the power of dialogue, putting them on a par with Shakespeare's. He also admired her realism, and wrote in his journal of 14 March 1826:

> [Miss Austen] had a talent for describing the involvements and feelings and characters of ordinary life which is to me the most wonderful I have ever met with. [She had an] exquisite touch, which renders ordinary commonplace things and characters interesting, from the truth of the description and the sentiment.

Richard Whateley also praised Austen's characterisation and its distinctiveness as 'hardly exceeded by Shakespeare himself' (1821). The Prince Regent kept a set of her works in every one of his residences, and *Pride and Prejudice* went through three printings during Austen's lifetime.

The next generation

In her own lifetime, no one disputed her judgements and standards. However, with the coming of social change and decay, religious doubt, the questioning of the position of women, and the publication of *The Communist Manifesto* by Karl Marx in 1848, her work began to be seen differently. Thomas Carlyle (1795–1881) dismissed her novels as 'mere dish-washings!' The best-known nineteenth-century female writers, Charlotte Brontë, Elizabeth Barrett Browning and George Eliot, were all unimpressed by Austen's work, which they described as limited. She was not generally palatable to post-Romantic readers because of the lack of overtly described passion and the apparent conformity to social regulation of her characters; they perceived her as championing classical virtues and neglecting matters of the heart. Austen criticism of the Victorian period always puts emphasis on what is perceived to be the littleness, restriction and domesticity in her works. Brontë said of *Pride and Prejudice*:

> ...a commonplace face; a carefully fenced, highly cultivated garden, [...] but no glance of a bright, vivid physiognomy, no open country, no fresh air, no blue hill, no bonny beck. I should hardly like to live with her ladies and gentlemen, in their elegant but confined houses.

As a result of the publication by her nephew, James Edward Austen-Leigh, of his *A Memoir of Jane Austen* (1870), public interest in Austen grew and she became more widely known, especially in America. He praises her gift of the 'intuitive perception of genius', but also created a bland legend around her, which probably did her a disservice: 'of events her life was singularly barren: few changes and no great crises ever broke the smooth current of its course [...] There was in her nothing eccentric or angular; no ruggedness of temper; no singularity of manner...' However, what author and critic (and father of Virginia Woolf) Leslie Stephen (1832–1904) later described as 'Austenolotry' developed as a result.

Early twentieth century

At the turn of the century, Henry James was surprisingly dismissive of Austen's talents, as a head rather than a heart man himself, and one whose own works seems to have distinct similarities to Austen's in setting, plot and style. He thought the issues she dealt with were not grand enough, and that there was too much 'light felicity'. Some of his comments were kinder than many of those of the previous period, but still patronising, as in his praise of her 'little master-strokes of imagination'. However, A. C. Bradley's essay of 1911 was a milestone on the road to a serious academic approach to Austen studies; he was the first to draw attention to her ties to Dr Johnson, to her being a moralist as well as a humorist, and to her use of the ironic authorial viewpoint, which allows us to realise how different things are from the way the characters see them. For the next few years appreciation for her subtlety gained ground.

Austen found favour with the Bloomsbury group, who were a group of artists based in the area of London around the British Museum from about 1905 until the outbreak of the Second World War. They reacted against the Victorian critical views of Austen, which they found too earnest, and because of their own writerly emphasis on personal relationships they approved of hers. E. M. Forster (1879–1970) was one of her most ardent admirers and disciples; he lamented to a correspondent that had she lived to 90 she could have written 12 more books. He discusses her fulsomely in his critical works *Aspects of the Novel* (1927), *Abinger Harvest* (1936) and *Two Cheers for Democracy* (1951). He was a sympathetic reconciler of head and heart, the motto of his novel *Howard's End* (1910) being 'only connect'. He said in an interview in 1953 that he had learned from Austen 'the possibilities of domestic humour', which he put to good use in his own social comedies. He is also known for his spirited, independent heroines.

R. W. Chapman's edited edition of *The Novels of Jane Austen* (1933), following his publication of her remaining letters in 1932, was a crucial turning point for her reputation. This was also partly due to Rudyard Kipling's short story 'The Janeites', which had begun an Austen cult when it was first published in 1924, and again in 1936, one based on the snobbish and elitist contention that the masses did not properly understand Austen. Many people think that Kipling invented the word 'Janeite' when he wrote about a group of British soldiers in the First World War who found relief from the horrors of war in 38Austen's work. However, the first appearance of the word in print (with the slightly different spelling of 'Janite') was in a preface to an 1894 edition of *Pride and Prejudice* written by George Edward Bateman Saintsbury, who used the term to refer to Jane's devoted fans. Early Janeites such as Saintsbury jealously guarded the image of Austen propagated by Henry Austen and James Edward Austen-Leigh: the demure, proper spinster who lived quietly in the country while penning her 'bits of ivory'. This was the first period during which she enjoyed a significant male readership and following, and she would have been especially surprised to find that she had found her way into the hearts of common soldiers, at least fictional ones, who said such things as: 'You take it from me, Brethren, there's no one to touch Jane when you're in a tight place. Gawd bless 'er, whoever she was.'

In 1939 Mary Lascelles published the first book-length critical study, *Jane Austen and her Art*. The following year an essay by the academic psychologist D. W. Harding, 'Regular hatred: an aspect of the work of Jane Austen', was first published in *Scrutiny*. He attacks the established notion that she was a kindly writer by analysing her use of satire, asserting that she was an intelligent and sensitive woman who found it almost intolerable to live among people less acute of mind and feeling than herself. In fact, he says, she hated such people, but since society would not allow her to express her hatred directly, she wrote novels as an outlet through which she could articulate her contempt for her inferiors and for the society that protected them. It signalled a move away from the Janeite camp and towards the Freudian one, drawing attention to the **Electra complex** whereby the heroine hates her mother, loves her father, rejects a suitor who is the opposite of her father and accepts a lover who can be a father-substitute. *Pride and Prejudice* was at an all-time low in the popularity league table of her novels in the late 1930s, but from then it began working its way up again as it was rediscovered through the new critical readings and the Hollywood film of 1940.

Late twentieth century onwards

Austen scholarship became more divided in the latter part of the twentieth century, when, fuelled by a wave of new film adaptations, popular interest in her work exploded. Marxists either rejected her for being bourgeois or tried to claim her as a pre-Marxian Marxist (as feminists have tried to claim her as a pre-feminist feminist) who exposes the economic basis of social behaviour.

The Janeites continued to apotheosise propriety and elegance as incarnated in the person and novels of Austen until the end of the century, most notably through the enthusiasm of Lord David Cecil, who lived until 1986.

Most writers through the ages have felt obliged to pronounce on Austen. There remains a perceived schism in Austen biography and criticism: fans who will not let go of the early memoirs by family members and continue to see her as a pious parson's daughter and the epitome of the conservatism of rural England, and critics who portray her as a cynic and satirist with a vicious tongue and poison pen. There is a world of difference between decorous lady author only interested in courtship, and social critic with a suppressed anger and subversive intent. Austen distrusted extremes in real life, and she would presumably tell us to apply common sense and find a

balanced position between the two. The last word can go to W. H. Auden (1907–73), who found her preoccupation with money quite shocking and who neatly expresses the contradiction in her reputation in his poem 'Letter to Lord Byron':

> It makes me most uncomfortable to see
> An English spinster of the middle class
> Describe the amorous effects of 'brass',
> Reveal so frankly and with such sobriety
> The economic basis of society.

Chapter summaries

Chapter 1

The news that a wealthy young gentleman named Charles Bingley has rented the manor known as Netherfield Park causes a great stir in the neighbouring village of Longbourn, especially in the Bennet household, with its five unmarried daughters. Mrs Bennet insists that their father call on the newcomer immediately. He pretends not to intend to do so.

Chapter 2

Mr Bennet tells the family that he has been to visit Bingley, and they are overjoyed.

Chapter 3

Bingley returns the visit and is invited to dinner shortly afterward, but he is called away to London. Soon, however, he returns to Netherfield with his two sisters, his brother-in-law, and a friend named Darcy, all of whom he takes to the Meryton ball, which the Bennet sisters attend with their mother. The eldest daughter, Jane, dances twice with Bingley, who describes her, within Elizabeth's hearing, as 'the most beautiful creature' he has ever beheld. Bingley suggests that Darcy dance with Elizabeth, but Darcy refuses peremptorily. Elizabeth takes an immediate dislike to Darcy, shared by the rest of the neighbourhood.

Chapter 4

Jane and Elizabeth discuss the ball and Elizabeth realises that Jane has fallen for Bingley, and even has a good word for his haughty sisters. We are told that Darcy found the inhabitants of Meryton to be lacking in beauty and fashion.

Chapter 5

The Bennet females discuss the ball the morning after with their neighbours and friends, the Lucas females. They predict that something will come of Bingley's preference for Jane. They criticise Darcy for being too proud and not willing to converse.

Chapter 6

Bingley continues to pay attention to Jane, whom Elizabeth decides is 'in a way to be very much in love', but Charlotte warns Elizabeth that Jane is concealing it too well and that Bingley may lose interest. Darcy finds himself becoming attracted to Elizabeth and he listens to her conversations with others. At a party at the Lucas house, Sir William attempts to persuade Elizabeth and Darcy to dance together, but Elizabeth refuses. Darcy tells Bingley's unmarried sister, who is interested in him herself, that 'Miss Elizabeth Bennet' is now the object of his admiration.

Chapter 7

The reader learns that Mr Bennet's property is entailed and cannot be inherited by his daughters. His two youngest children, Catherine and Lydia, begin a series of visits to their mother's sister, Mrs Philips, in the town of Meryton, to flirt with and gossip about the militia now stationed there. A note arrives inviting Jane to Netherfield Park for a day. Mrs Bennet and Elizabeth conspire to send Jane by horse rather than coach, knowing that it will rain and that Jane will consequently have to spend the night at Bingley's house. Unfortunately, their plan works out too well: Jane is soaked, falls ill, and is forced to remain at Netherfield as an invalid. Elizabeth goes to visit her, on foot through mud. When she arrives with a dirty petticoat and untidy hair she causes quite a stir. Jane insists that her sister stay the night, and the Bingleys consent.

Chapter 8

That evening, while Elizabeth is sitting with Jane, the Bingley sisters make fun of Elizabeth's wild appearance and the Bennets in general. Darcy and Bingley defend them, though Darcy concedes that their lack of wealth and family connections make them poor marriage prospects. When Elizabeth returns to the room, the discussion turns to Darcy's library at his ancestral home of Pemberley, and then to Darcy's opinion of what constitutes an 'accomplished woman'. Elizabeth argues that he is too demanding.

Chapter 9

The next day, Mrs Bennet arrives with Lydia and Kitty to visit Jane. To Elizabeth's dismay, Mrs Bennet tries to convince Bingley to remain at Netherfield and shows off about the locality, causing embarrassment to her family and smirks from the Bingley sisters. Lydia gets Bingley to agree to hold a ball at Netherfield when Jane is recovered.

Chapter 10

In the evening, Elizabeth observes Miss Bingley piling compliments upon Darcy as he writes to his sister. The conversation turns prophetically to Bingley's impetuous behaviour and an argument over the virtue of accepting the advice of friends.

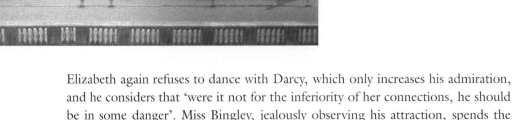

Elizabeth again refuses to dance with Darcy, which only increases his admiration, and he considers that 'were it not for the inferiority of her connections, he should be in some danger'. Miss Bingley, jealously observing his attraction, spends the following day making fun of Elizabeth's family, and the idea of it being connected to his, and continues to try to impress him herself.

Chapter 11

Miss Bingley spends the following evening in similar fashion, trying to attract Darcy's attention: first by reading, then by criticising the foolishness of balls, and finally by walking about the room. Only when she asks Elizabeth to walk with her, however, does Darcy look up. The two women discuss the possibility of finding something to ridicule in his character.

Chapter 12

The next morning, Elizabeth writes to her mother to say that she and Jane are ready to return home. Mrs Bennet wishes Jane to stay longer with Bingley, so refuses to send the carriage. Elizabeth, anxious to be away, insists on borrowing Bingley's carriage and she and her sister leave Netherfield. Darcy is glad to see them go, as Elizabeth attracts him 'more than he liked' considering her unsuitability as a prospect for matrimony.

Chapter 13

Mr Bennet informs his wife of an imminent visit from the Mr William Collins, who will inherit Mr Bennet's property, and reads his letter mockingly. Mr Collins arrives at Longbourn and apologises insincerely for being entitled to it, while simultaneously admiring the house that will one day be his.

Chapter 14

At dinner, Mr Collins lavishes praise on his patroness, Lady Catherine de Bourgh. After the meal, he refuses to read from a novel and takes up a book of sermons instead. Lydia becomes so bored that she interrupts his reading with more gossip about the soldiers. Mr Collins is offended and abandons the reading.

Chapter 15

Mr Collins has been told by his patroness to find a wife, and when Mrs Bennet hints that Jane may soon be engaged, he fixes his attention on Elizabeth. He accompanies the sisters to Meryton, where they encounter one of Lydia's officer friends, Mr Denny. Denny introduces his friend George Wickham, who has just joined the militia, and the young women find Wickham charming. While they converse, Darcy and Bingley pass by and Elizabeth notices that Wickham and Darcy are extremely cold to each other. Darcy and Bingley depart, and the company pays a visit to Mrs Philips, who invites the Bennets and Mr Collins to dine at her house the following evening. The girls persuade her to invite Wickham as well.

Chapter 16

At the Philips' dinner party, Wickham is the centre of attention; he tells Elizabeth that he had planned on entering the ministry, rather than the militia, but was unable to do so because he lacked money. He says that although Darcy's father had intended to provide for him, Darcy used a loophole in the will to keep the money for himself. Elizabeth, who instinctively likes and trusts Wickham, accepts his story immediately. Wickham also tells her that Darcy is Lady Catherine de Bourgh's nephew, and describes the aunt as 'dictatorial and insolent'. Elizabeth's antipathy to Darcy has been strengthened.

Chapter 17

Elizabeth expresses these feelings to Jane the next day. Jane defends Darcy, saying that there is probably a misunderstanding between the two men, but Elizabeth will have none of it. When Bingley invites the neighbourhood to a ball the following Tuesday, she looks forward to seeing Wickham. Unfortunately, she is forced to promise the first two dances to Mr Collins.

Chapter 18

Much to Elizabeth's dismay, Wickham does not attend the ball. Denny tells Elizabeth and Lydia that Darcy's presence keeps Wickham away from Netherfield. Elizabeth's unhappiness increases during two clumsy dances with Mr Collins and reaches its peak when she finds herself dancing with Darcy. Their conversation is awkward, especially when she mentions Wickham, a subject Darcy clearly wishes to avoid. At the end of the dance, Elizabeth encounters Miss Bingley, who warns her not to trust Wickham. Elizabeth assumes that Bingley's sister is only being spiteful, however, and chooses to ignore the warning. Jane then tells her sister that she has asked Bingley for information about Wickham, but everything Bingley knows about the officer comes from Darcy and is therefore (in Elizabeth's mind) suspect. Mr Collins, meanwhile, realises that Darcy is related to his patroness, Lady Catherine, and insists on introducing himself, which is greeted with contempt by Darcy. At supper, Mrs Bennet discusses the hoped-for union of Bingley and Jane so loudly that Darcy hears. At the end of the meal, Mary performs a terrible song for the company, and Mr Collins delivers a speech of absurd pomposity. Elizabeth feels that her family has completely embarrassed itself.

Chapter 19

Mr Collins proposes marriage to Elizabeth, assuming that she will be overjoyed. She turns him down and Mrs Bennet, who regards a match between her daughter and Mr Collins as advantageous because of the entail, is furious.

Chapter 20

Mrs Bennet tries in vain to get her husband to order Elizabeth to marry Collins. The latter withdraws his suit.

Chapter 21

Elizabeth encounters Wickham in Meryton. He apologises for his absence from the ball and walks her home, where Elizabeth introduces him to her parents. That same day, a letter arrives for Jane from Miss Bingley, informing her that Bingley and his party are returning to the city indefinitely and implying that Bingley plans to marry Darcy's sister, Georgiana. Elizabeth comforts Jane, telling her that this turn of events is all Miss Bingley's doing, not her brother's, and that Bingley will return to Netherfield.

Chapter 22

Charlotte comes to tell Elizabeth that she has accepted a proposal from Mr Collins. Elizabeth is shocked at her friend's lack of taste, despite Charlotte's insistence that the match is the best for which she could hope at her age.

Chapter 23

Mrs Bennet is first incredulous and then furious to learn that Charlotte will be the future mistress of her house. As the days go by with no word from Bingley, Jane's marriage prospects begin to fade. Mr Collins returns for another stay at Longbourn, abandoning his parish in Kent.

[End of volume 1]

Chapter 24

Miss Bingley sends another letter, this one praising the beauty and charm of Darcy's sister. The letter further states that Bingley will remain in London all winter, putting an end to the Bennets' hopes that he might return to Netherfield. Elizabeth is very upset by this news on her sister's behalf and complains to Jane that people lack 'merit or sense', referring to Bingley for abandoning Jane and to Charlotte for agreeing to marry Mr Collins.

Chapter 25

Mrs Bennet's brother and sister-in-law, the Gardiners, comes to stay with the family for Christmas. Sympathising with Jane's sadness, they invite Jane to accompany them back to London when they finish their visit, hoping that a change in scenery might raise her spirits. In the course of evenings spent with various friends and military officers, Mrs Gardiner notices that Elizabeth and Wickham show a definite preference for each other and is alarmed by it, knowing Wickham to be seriously interested only in women with a fortune.

Chapter 26

Mrs Gardiner warns Elizabeth that Wickham's need of money makes him an unsuitable marriage prospect. After Jane and the Gardiners depart for London, Mr Collins returns to Hertfordshire for his wedding. Elizabeth reluctantly promises to visit Charlotte after her marriage. Meanwhile, Jane's letters from London recount how she called on Miss Bingley and how the latter was cold to her and visited her only briefly in return. Jane believes that Bingley's sister views her as an obstacle to her brother's marrying Georgiana Darcy (a match which would help Miss Bingley to pursue her own cause of capturing Darcy). Elizabeth admits to Mrs Gardiner that Wickham has turned his attentions to a Miss King, a recent beneficiary of £10,000.

Chapter 27

Elizabeth travels with Sir William and Maria Lucas to visit Charlotte in her new home in Kent. On the way, they spend a night in London with Jane and the Gardiners. Elizabeth and her aunt speak about Wickham's attempts to win over Miss King; Mrs Gardiner is critical of his mercenary attitude, but Elizabeth defends his prudence in desiring to marry for money (although she did not allow the same licence to Charlotte). Before Elizabeth leaves London, the Gardiners invite her to accompany them on a tour of the north of England, and she gratefully accepts.

Chapter 28

When Elizabeth arrives in Mr Collins's parish of Hunsford she is greeted enthusiastically as someone to impress. Mr Collins shows off his house. Miss de Bourgh invites them all to dine at Rosings.

Chapter 29

The de Bourgh mansion awes even Sir William Lucas with its grandeur. At dinner, Lady Catherine dominates the conversation and finds fault with the upbringing of the Bennet girls.

Chapter 30

Sir William departs after a week, satisfied that Charlotte is well established and contented. Darcy and a cousin named Colonel Fitzwilliam visit their aunt at Rosings. When Mr Collins pays his respects, the two men accompany him back to his parsonage and visit briefly with Elizabeth and Charlotte.

Chapter 31

Another invitation to Rosings follows, and Colonel Fitzwilliam pays special attention to Elizabeth during the dinner. After the meal, she plays the piano and makes fun of Darcy, informing Colonel Fitzwilliam of his bad behaviour at the Meryton ball, at which he refused to dance with her.

Chapter 32

The next day, Darcy visits the parsonage and tells Elizabeth that Bingley is unlikely to spend much of his time at Netherfield Park in the future. The rest of their conversation is awkward, and when Darcy departs Charlotte declares that he must be in love with Elizabeth, or he would never have called in such an odd manner.

Chapter 33

Elizabeth has a conversation with Colonel Fitzwilliam, who mentions that Darcy claims to have recently saved a friend from an imprudent marriage. Elizabeth is certain that Darcy is the agent of her sister's unhappiness, and refuses to go to Rosings to drink tea in order to avoid him.

Chapter 34

Darcy finds Elizabeth alone at the parsonage and abruptly declares his love for her. His proposal of marriage dwells upon her social inferiority, and Elizabeth's initially polite rejection turns into an angry accusation when he admits that he interfered in the Jane/Bingley relationship. She then repeats Wickham's accusations and declares that Darcy is proud and selfish, and that marriage to him would be unthinkable. Darcy grimly departs.

Chapter 35

The following day Elizabeth takes a walk and Darcy gives her a letter that she immediately reads. In it Darcy tries to defend himself for breaking up Bingley's romance with Jane, in order to spare his friend social embarrassment, by saying that he did not believe her to have been sufficiently involved to be heartbroken. In relation to Wickham, the letter states that Darcy did provide for him after his father's death and that the root of their quarrel lay in an attempt by Wickham to elope with Darcy's sister, Georgiana, in the hope of obtaining her fortune.

Chapter 36

Elizabeth is stunned by these revelations, and wanders for a long while considering them. Although she dismisses Darcy's excuse for his influence over Bingley, his account of Wickham's doings causes her to reappraise the officer and decide that she was probably wrong to trust him. Her feelings toward Darcy suddenly enter into flux.

Chapter 37

Darcy and Colonel Fitzwilliam depart from Rosings. Elizabeth informs Lady Catherine that she too must leave the parsonage, despite the latter's insistence that she stay another two weeks.

Chapter 38

Elizabeth says farewell to Charlotte, and she and Maria travel to the Gardiners in London and meet up with Jane.

Chapter 39

The three girls return home, after being met by Kitty and Lydia in their father's coach. Lydia is full of the news that the regiment is being sent to Brighton for the summer, and that Wickham is no longer interested in Miss King. Mr and Mrs Bennet welcome their daughters home, and the Lucases come for dinner. Lydia plans to persuade her parents to let her go to Brighton too.

Chapter 40

Elizabeth tells Jane about Darcy's proposal and the truth about Wickham. They debate whether to expose him publicly, ultimately deciding against it. Meanwhile, Mrs Bennet continues to bemoan the loss of Bingley as a husband for Jane, and voices her displeasure at the happy marriage of Charlotte and Mr Collins, the future owners of Longbourn.

Chapter 41

Lydia is invited to spend the summer in Brighton by the wife of Colonel Forster, much to Kitty's chagrin. Mr Bennet refuses Elizabeth's advice that he should forbid her to go, since he assumes that the colonel will keep her out of trouble. Elizabeth sees Wickham once more before his regiment departs, and they discuss Darcy in a guarded manner.

Chapter 42

Kitty is distraught to see the soldiers leave and not be allowed to go with them, along with Lydia. Elizabeth accompanies the Gardiners on a tour of Derbyshire, agreeing to visit Darcy's estate only when she is assured that he is not in residence.

[End of volume 2]

Chapter 43

Elizabeth tours the beautiful house of Pemberley with the Gardiners, imagining what it would be like to be mistress there. The housekeeper shows them portraits of Darcy and Wickham and relates that Darcy, in his youth, was 'the sweetest, most generous-hearted boy in the world', and that he is still the kindest of masters. Elizabeth is surprised to hear such an agreeable description of a man she considers unbearably arrogant. While they are still in the grounds, Darcy himself suddenly appears, behaves politely, and joins them in their walk. He explains that he has returned early to prepare for guests, which include his sister, whom he would like to present to Elizabeth. After Darcy leaves them, the Gardiners comment on his good looks and good manners, so strikingly divergent from the account of Darcy's character that Elizabeth has given them.

Chapter 44

The next day, Darcy and Georgiana, who is very shy, visit Elizabeth at her inn, followed by Bingley. Elizabeth and the Gardiners, who perceive that Darcy is in love with their niece, are invited to dine at Pemberley.

Chapter 45

The following morning, Elizabeth and Mrs Gardiner visit Pemberley to call on Miss Darcy. Bingley's sisters are both present and when Darcy enters the room, Miss Bingley makes a spiteful comment to Elizabeth about the loss to her family of the soldiers. Elizabeth dodges the subject of Wickham. After the guests depart, Miss Bingley attempts to criticise Elizabeth to Darcy, but he replies that he now considers Elizabeth 'one of the handsomest women of my acquaintance'.

Chapter 46

When Elizabeth returns to her inn, she finds two letters from Jane: the first relates that Lydia has eloped with Wickham, the second that there is no word from the couple and that they may not be married yet, so their father has gone to London to find them. Elizabeth panics, realising that if Wickham does not marry her youngest sister, the reputations of both Lydia and the entire family will be ruined. As Elizabeth is about to rush out to find the Gardiners, Darcy appears and she explains to him the situation. She and Darcy blame themselves for not exposing Wickham. The Gardiners take Elizabeth home to Longbourn immediately.

Chapter 47

On the way home, Mr Gardiner attempts to reassure his niece that Wickham will certainly marry Lydia because he will not want his own career and reputation ruined. Elizabeth replies by telling them generally about Wickham's past behaviour, without revealing the details of his liaison with Darcy's sister. At Longbourn Mrs Bennet is hysterical, blaming Colonel Forster for not taking care of her daughter. In private, Jane assures Elizabeth that there was no way anyone could have known about their sister's attachment to Wickham. They examine the letter that Lydia left for Colonel Forster's wife, in which she looks forward to signing her name 'Lydia Wickham'.

Chapter 48

Mr Gardiner follows Mr Bennet to London and writes to Longbourn a few days later with the news that the search for the couple in hotels has been unsuccessful so far. A letter arrives from Mr Collins that accuses the Bennets of poor parenting and notes that Lydia's behaviour reflects badly on the family as a whole. More time passes before Mr Gardiner writes to say that attempts to trace Wickham through friends and family have failed, and that Mr Bennet is returning home.

Chapter 49

Two days after Mr Bennet returns to Longbourn, Mr Gardiner writes to tell him that Wickham and Lydia have been found and that Wickham will marry her if the Bennets will guarantee him a small income. Mr Bennet gladly acquiesces, deciding that marriage to a scoundrel is better than a ruined reputation. The Bennets assume that the Gardiners have paid Wickham a sizable amount to get him to agree to the wedding, and that they owe a deep debt to their relatives. Mrs Bennet rises from her bed and is deliriously happy at having Lydia married, even under such circumstances, but is peeved when her husband refuses to allow Wickham and Lydia to visit, or to provide her with money to purchase clothes.

Chapter 50

Elizabeth realises that her opinion of Darcy has changed so completely that if he were to propose to her again, she would accept. She understands, however, that, given Lydia's shameful elopement and the addition of Wickham to the Bennet family, another proposal seems extremely unlikely. Mr Gardiner writes to Mr Bennet again to inform him that Wickham has accepted a commission in the north of England. Lydia asks to be allowed to visit her family before she goes north with her new husband. After persuasion by Jane and Elizabeth, Mr Bennet allows the newlyweds to call at their home.

Chapter 51

The ten-day visit is difficult; Lydia and Wickham are oblivious to all the trouble they have caused. Lydia describes her wedding and lets slip to Jane and Elizabeth that Darcy was in the church. Elizabeth is amazed and sends a letter to Mrs Gardiner asking for an explanation.

Chapter 52

Mrs Gardiner replies to Elizabeth that it was Darcy who found Lydia and Wickham, and Darcy who paid the money that facilitated the marriage, but that he did not wish it to become known. She drops hints that Darcy did it because of his love for Elizabeth. Her surprise is immense, and she is unsure whether to be upset or pleased. She has a final conversation with Wickham in which she lets it be known that she knows the truth about him.

Chapter 53

After Wickham and Lydia depart for their new home in the north, news arrives that Bingley is returning to Netherfield for a few weeks. Mr Bennet refuses to visit him.

Three days after his arrival, however, Bingley visits the Bennets, accompanied by Darcy. Mrs Bennet is overly attentive to Bingley and quite rude to Darcy, completely unaware that he was the one who saved Lydia. Before departing, the gentlemen promise to dine at Longbourn soon.

Chapter 54

Darcy and Bingley dine at Longbourn; Bingley places himself next to Jane and pays her much attention, but Darcy and Elizabeth are not able to converse.

Chapter 55

Bingley visits the Bennets a few days later, and eagerly accepts a dinner invitation for the following day. He calls so early that the women are not dressed. After the meal, Mrs Bennet manages, clumsily, to leave Bingley alone with Jane, but he does not propose. The following day, however, Bingley goes shooting with Mr Bennet and stays for dinner. After the meal, when he finds himself alone with Jane again, he tells her that he will ask Mr Bennet for permission to marry her. Mr Bennet happily agrees and Jane tells Elizabeth that she is 'the happiest creature in the world'. She has learnt that Bingley had no idea that she was in London over the winter, because his sisters were determined to keep him away from her.

Chapter 56

A week after Bingley and Jane become engaged, Lady Catherine de Bourgh appears unannounced at Longbourn, wanting to speak with Elizabeth. They walk in the hermitage, where Lady Catherine informs Elizabeth that she has heard a rumour (via the gossiping Lucases) that she and Darcy are planning to marry. Such a notion, Lady Catherine insists, is ridiculous, given Elizabeth's low station in life and the tacit engagement of Darcy to her own daughter. Elizabeth conceals her surprise at this news and acts very coolly toward Lady Catherine. She admits that she and Darcy are not engaged but, despite the noblewoman's demands, refuses to promise not to enter into an engagement to him in the future. Lady Catherine leaves, furious and frustrated, and Elizabeth keeps their conversation a secret.

Chapter 57

A letter arrives from Mr Collins for Mr Bennet which suggests that an engagement between Darcy and Elizabeth is imminent and warning against it. Mr Bennet mocks the idea with Elizabeth, who is unable to join in the joke.

Chapter 58

Darcy again comes to stay with Bingley at Netherfield. The two friends visit the Bennets, and everyone takes a walk together. Elizabeth and Darcy lag behind, and when they are alone, Elizabeth thanks him for his generosity in saving Lydia's good name. Darcy replies that he did so only because Lydia is her sister. He then says that his feelings toward her have not changed since his proposal. Elizabeth tells him that her own feelings have changed and that she is now willing to marry him.

Chapter 59

Elizabeth tells a stunned Jane that she has agreed to marry Darcy. The next day, Darcy and Elizabeth walk together again, and that night Darcy goes to Mr Bennet to ask him for his consent to the match. Mr Bennet needs Elizabeth to convince him that she does indeed care for Darcy, and she tells him how Darcy paid off Wickham. Mrs Bennet learns of her second daughter's engagement and is suitably ecstatic.

Chapter 60

Darcy and Elizabeth discuss how their love began and how it developed. Darcy writes to inform Lady Catherine of his engagement, while Elizabeth communicates the situation to her own aunt. Mr Bennet sends a gloating letter to Mr Collins. The Collins come to Lucas Lodge to escape an angry Lady Catherine.

Chapter 61

After the weddings, Bingley purchases an estate near Pemberley, and the Bennet sisters visit one another frequently. Kitty is kept away from Lydia and her bad influence, and she matures greatly by spending time at her elder sisters' homes. Lydia and Wickham remain incorrigible, asking Darcy for money and visiting the Bingleys so frequently that even the good-humoured Bingley grows tired of them. Elizabeth becomes great friends with Georgiana, and Lady Catherine eventually accepts the marriage and visits her nephew and his wife at Pemberley. Darcy and Elizabeth continue to consider the Gardiners close friends, grateful for the fact that they brought Elizabeth to Pemberley the first time and helped to bring the couple together.

Character notes

Elizabeth Bennet

All we know of her appearance is that she has a pair of fine dark eyes, which render her 'uncommonly intelligent', and a slight figure. Her family calls her 'Lizzy', her friends and neighbours call her 'Eliza', and the narrator calls her 'Elizabeth'. Frank, assertive, sensitive, spirited: these are all adjectives that can be used of the second Bennet daughter, not yet 'one and twenty'. She is the only sister who has 'quickness' of mind, which is appreciated by her father but a cause of puzzlement to her mother, to whom she is 'the least dear to her of all her children' because she is a 'very

headstrong foolish girl'. She is the lens through which the action and the other characters of the novel are seen, and it is a lens with a flaw: a desire to be thought witty, a 'lively playful disposition, which delighted in anything ridiculous', and a 'lively imagination [which] soon settled it all' are attractive traits but also liabilities, and ones that lead to faulty judgement. It is 'her temper to be happy' (p. 231), however, so she is a true comedy heroine.

Elizabeth is secretive on several occasions, even towards Jane and her father. She is far from perfect, and makes enemies because of what is perceived by some to be 'conceit and impertinence', and because of her sarcasm (she tells Lady Catherine that being slighted and despised by the latter would be 'heavy misfortunes' p. 336). She is too sure of her own judgements; she tells Jane, who is more right than she is about Darcy, that 'one knows exactly what to think'. She is critical, intolerant and harsh in her judgements of others, believing, for instance, that Charlotte has disgraced herself by accepting, of necessity, the only proposal ever made or likely to be made to her, and that the other Lucas sister is 'empty-headed' and 'had nothing to say that could be worth hearing'. Her outburst when she learns of Wickham's transference of attentions is sarcastic and extreme — 'I am sick of them all' — and her aunt reprimands her to 'Take care, Lizzy'. She is, like her mother, capable of uncharitable reactions, such as when she exclaims that Lady Lucas should have stayed at home rather than offer her condolences and services during the Lydia crisis, assuming that she had come to triumph over the Bennets. Ironically, she often behaves like her mother, another occasion being earlier in Chapter 47 when she is fear-mongering over Lydia's situation and leaping to the most negative conclusion. She learns clear-sightedness through her errors, which arise from false assumptions, i.e. prejudice, but also from pride because she is piqued by Darcy's rudeness about her at the assembly room ball. Her two other reasons for disliking Darcy are that he allegedly disinherited her favourite, Wickham, and that he interfered with her sister's relationship with Bingley. Like Marianne Dashwood, she 'was born to an extraordinary fate. She was born to discover the falsehood of her own opinions, and to counteract, by her conduct, her most favourite maxims'.

Fitzwilliam Darcy

Aged 28, owner of Pemberley Hall, Derbyshire, since his father's death five years previously, and of a house in London, he possesses a French aristocratic name (originally d'Arcy) and noble lineage, and a 'very satirical eye', which Elizabeth finds intimidating. (Fitzwilliam is, incidentally, a name that the young Jane Austen imagined for her own future husband). He also has an additional £10,000 a year, making him relatively very rich. He is 'ashamed of his aunt's ill breeding', which is to his credit, as is his lack of interest in marrying his cousin, her daughter Anne, or his friend's sister, Caroline Bingley, simply for dynastic reasons. Family loyalty is strong, however, where his sister and ward, Georgiana, is concerned, and he is described as 'the best of brothers'. Even

Wickham allows that Darcy is 'a kind and careful guardian of his sister' and is 'liberal-minded, just, sincere, rational, honourable, and perhaps agreeable' — all the attributes which Austen approves of. However, Darcy persuades Bingley that Jane Bennet is not to be viewed as a serious marriage prospect, genuinely believing that she is indifferent to him, and this is the main obstacle to his winning Elizabeth. Ill at ease with strangers, pride is his failing and cause of his prejudice against the entire Bennet family, although only two of the sisters, one of the aunts and uncles, and one of the parents are guilty of a 'total want of propriety'. Mr Collins is also a family member and a further obstacle to Elizabeth's social aspirations. Darcy also prides himself on his inflexibility: 'My good opinion once lost is lost for ever.' He is considered intellectual by the Bingleys for being a reader and using 'words of four syllables'.

Mr Bennet

The head of the family of six females is irresponsible as a father and husband. That Longbourn will be lost to the family on his death, though not his fault, reflects badly on him as he has made no other provision for them. Although his ready wit makes him an appealing character, and he redeems himself somewhat at the end by at least recognising his negligence and accepting the blame for Lydia's elopement, he spoils the effect of this by saying immediately afterwards that it will not make a lasting impression. He regards his children and his acquaintance as an author would his fictional creations: commenting on and criticising them drolly but without apparent personal feeling or involvement in their lives and fates. His creator summarises him as a 'mixture of quick parts, sarcastic humour, reserve and caprice'. This is not an admirable set of qualities, but he shares them with his favourite daughter, Elizabeth. He hates London, which is to his credit in Austen's world of suspicion of the metropolis and insistence on the delights of the countryside, but loves his library too much. He has a sadistic streak and enjoys thwarting and baiting his wife and witnessing her disappointments, is amused by his daughters being crossed in love, and values his son-in-law Wickham because of his 'impudence and hypocrisy'. He fails in his paternal responsibility to 'restrain the wild giddiness of his youngest daughters', preferring to laugh at them rather than 'exert himself', and Elizabeth has no illusions about 'the impropriety of her father's behaviour as a husband' (p. 228) or the moral inadequacy of his 'philosophic composure'. He represents the deadly sin of sloth because of his natural 'indolence'. His rage at Lydia — whom he allowed to go to Brighton against Elizabeth's advice — has to be overcome by the reasoning of Jane and Elizabeth, as if he were the child and they the parents, and tact and wisdom seem to have eluded him.

Mrs Bennet

Married for 23 years, the mother of the five girls must be in her early forties. She fancies that she suffers from her 'nerves', is 'invariably silly', completely

humourless, and a gossip who competes with the neighbours. She is also a tedious hypochondriac, which causes her husband to win sympathy for being long-suffering. Her vulgarity and materialism are the cause of embarrassment and a handicap to Jane and Elizabeth's prospects. Thanks to her talking loudly and boastfully of the expected union between Jane and Bingley, Darcy is alerted to the danger to his friend and the need to remove him from the vicinity. Her failure to set a good example to her five daughters almost leads to Lydia's 'irremediable infamy' and the social disgrace of the whole family. She hypocritically blames her own irresponsibility in letting Lydia go to Brighton on the failure of Colonel Forster to supervise her. Her creator describes her as 'a woman of mean under-standing, little information, and uncertain temper', and as having 'weak under-standing and illiberal mind', which is damning criticism indeed. Her moods are 'violent', veering between the extremes of 'exuberance' and 'alarm'. As she is always wrong, the reader learns that the right opinion is always the opposite of whatever she says. Elizabeth she considers to be 'not a bit better than the others', being unable to appreciate her wit and intelligence; sometimes Lydia and sometimes Jane is 'beyond competition her favourite child' adding inconstancy and favouritism to her list of faults. Her illogicalities ('it is the first time we have ever had anything from him, except a few presents'; 'any friend of Mr Bingley's will always be welcome here [...] else I must say that I hate the very sight of him') and inconsistencies (she is afraid Mr Bennet will fight Wickham in a duel and be killed, but when she learns her husband is coming home, she asks 'Who is to fight Wickham...?') are the main source of comedy in the novel. One might have some sympathy for a women with five daughters to marry off, but we are not allowed to **empathise** with her because, as an unsatisfactory wife and mother 'incapable of exertion', she is one of the novel's major moral concerns.

Jane Bennet

Jane Bennet, aged 22, is often referred to as 'Miss Bennet', being the eldest daughter. She is considered, even by Darcy, as the prettiest of the sisters. She is trusting, unsceptical and passive to a degree some might call insipid, accepting without demur her abandonment by Bingley. Elizabeth tells her 'You never see a fault in anybody', which is more a failure of discernment than a gift of tolerance, since it entails being 'blind to the follies and nonsense of others' (p. 16). Though her 'mild and steady candour' is admirable, she reveals her inability to make judgements when she admits 'I know not what to think'. She refuses to believe that Caroline Bingley is capable 'of wilfully deceiving anyone' and insists on seeing everything and everyone 'in the best light', even after Lydia's disappearance. However, she is sometimes nearer the mark than Elizabeth, since she is free of both pride and prejudice; her being 'afraid of judging harshly' is a corrective to her sister's tendency to be overly critical. Jane is goodness personified, summed up as 'a sweet girl', and as such rather lacklustre; Darcy thinks she smiles too much, and Elizabeth says tellingly of her 'she only smiles, I laugh' (p. 361).

Mary Bennet

The only plain one in the family, the middle daughter spouts pompous platitudes: 'Dr Johnson mounted and stuffed' (Craik p. 75). She has 'neither genius nor taste' and her bookishness does not impress anyone, any more than her bad piano playing and singing, though she does not have enough self-knowledge to recognise this. As a female equivalent of Mr Collins, she speaks in risible platitudes and mixed metaphors: 'we must stem the tide of malice, and pour into the wounded bosoms of each other, the balm of sisterly consolation' (p. 274). That 'Mary wished to say something very sensible, but knew not how' (p. 9) shows the reader that her creator did not approve of learning in isolation without access to experience. She is a purely comic character, a **caricature** in fact, with no plot role to play, who exists only to amuse and to warn the reader of the dangers of cultivating traits deserving of mirth and undeserving of marriage.

Lydia Bennet

Only 15 years old, Lydia the flirt is proud of being the tallest though the youngest. She is described in the most derogatory terms: 'impertinent' and 'imprudent', 'self-willed and careless', guilty of 'wild volatility', 'wickedness', and 'ignorance and emptiness of mind'. She is incorrigible and irrational; she gives as her reason for buying an unattractive hat that 'there were two or three much uglier in the shop'. She is loud and indiscreet, not caring whether the servants can hear and asking Bingley for a ball, indifferent to the state of her sister's health; this prepares us for her moral irresponsibility in eloping with Wickham and not caring whether it brings disgrace on her family. She has already damaged her elder sisters' prospects by 'running after the officers'. She is her mother's favourite, being most like her in character, and has inherited from her the traits of being 'a most determined talker', 'always unguarded and often uncivil'. Everything is a joke or a laugh for her, as it is for her father. As she never listens to anyone she cannot ever learn anything or improve in any way. Careless about money as about everything else, she is also 'extremely fond of lottery tickets' and 'too eager in making bets', which is symbolic of her future gamble with her marriage and her life. Her body language is equally unrestrained and indecorous, as is shown by her giving a 'violent yawn' at the Netherfield ball. She is desperate to marry before she is 'three and twenty' and is not fussy which of the soldiers she catches. The dubious moral world of Brighton comprises earthly happiness for her. She is shameless to the end, when she begs for financial support from the husbands of her sisters.

Kitty (Catherine) Bennet

Two years older than Lydia, Kitty follows her younger sister in being a chaser of
men and looks likely to end up the same way. Their father calls them 'two of the
silliest girls in the country'; they can talk of 'nothing but officers' 'dazzling with
scarlet', and they are collectively 'ignorant, idle, and vain' and 'uncontrouled'.
The first thing we learn about Kitty is that she gets on her mother's nerves by
coughing, but this is to reflect on Mrs Bennet's irritability rather than on Kitty's
health. Her function is to be Lydia's partner and confidante, and to be a victim
of her dominant personality to show the effect of bad influence. She is described
as 'weak-spirited, irritable, and completely under Lydia's guidance', and
'affronted' by advice from her elder sisters. She is not able to go to Brighton with
Lydia, and takes this very badly by crying and sulking, which makes her very
different from her eldest sister Jane, who would not dream of complaining or
imposing her feelings on others and suffers in silence when her own marriage
hopes are dashed.

George Wickham

Son of the former steward to old Mr Darcy, Wickham is a Cambridge graduate, a
lieutenant in a county regiment and a gold-digger, and there is obviously the
suggestion of 'wicked' about his name. George, however, is a solidly reliable English
name, as in George Knightley (and Georgiana Darcy), so the combination suggests
his duplicity and his ability to fool even the most perceptive. His 'most gentlemanlike appearance' is deceptive, since beneath the showy blue and red coats he is
nothing but 'idle and frivolous gallantry'. Elizabeth is taken in by his appearance and
fine manners, on which he trades. His role is to add a sense of danger to the drawing
room; he is described as 'wild' on p. 237. Allegedly having intended to become a
clergyman in the Hampshire living of Kympton, he claims that Darcy has cheated
and impoverished him. In romantic fiction sons of servants have a troubled
relationship with the feudal family (e.g. *Atonement*). It turns out that he behaved
perfidiously to Georgiana Darcy, but in any case his verbal disclosures show
impropriety, as Elizabeth realises too late. Darcy accuses Wickham of 'vicious
propensities' and of having led 'a life of idleness and dissipation'. He is 'profligate',
'false and deceitful', and 'insinuating' (p. 270), 'imprudent and extravagant'
(p. 276). Money is his priority; Mary King's £10,000 a year attracts him away from
Elizabeth, and we learn from Darcy's housekeeper that he left debts behind him in
Derbyshire, and the same is true of his sojourn in Meryton. Owing money to
tradesmen was considered to be a serious character defect at the time, and one unbe-
fitting a gentleman. Furthermore, he is a 'gamester' with gambling debts owed in
Brighton of 'more than a thousand pounds'. He is the literary stereotype of the
gambler and serial seducer known as the 'rake' figure in eighteenth-century
literature.

The Reverend William Collins

Rector of Hunsford in Kent, he is cousin and heir (as the only male relative) to Mr Bennet, and was at one of the universities (i.e. Oxford or Cambridge), though his education has left little mark, given the deficiencies of his nature, and he is 'not a sensible man'; his 'stupidity' is demonstrated by, amongst other things, his dislike of novels and his inability to win a single point at whist. Though only 25, the reader has the impression he is much older because of his pomposity and formality. He makes himself 'absurd' by his constant fawning on his noble patroness and his mannered language, particularly his studied compliments and **clichés**. Incapable of real feeling, he transfers his attentions from Jane to Elizabeth, and then from Elizabeth to Charlotte, in a ridiculously short time when choosing the companion of his future life, as ordered by his patroness. He forms the link between Longbourn and Rosings, and unwittingly provides evidence of the objectionableness of Lady Catherine, as well as of the generally low social regard for the Bennet family. His rejected proposal to Elizabeth is a comic masterpiece that makes him seem ludicrous, but it is also a test of Elizabeth's judgement of character and views on marriage, and one that she passes to the delight of her father and the reader. He is satirised throughout the novel for being 'irksome' and does nothing for the image of the clergy, being 'a mixture of servility and self-importance' who, rather dubiously for a man of the cloth, plays cards for money, though very badly. He is presumptuous, introducing himself with 'impertinent freedom' to Darcy and invading Mr Bennet's study. His letter to Mr Bennet after Lydia's elopement is deeply offensive, crowned by his saying that it would be better if Lydia were dead, rejoicing that he didn't marry Elizabeth, and revealing his own hypocrisy and unsuitability to be a member of the church: 'You ought certainly to forgive them as a Christian, but never to admit them in your sight, or allow their names to be mentioned in your hearing.'

Charlotte Lucas

Charlotte is the eldest daughter of the Bennets' neighbours and rivals in Longbourn, and Elizabeth's closest friend. At the relatively advanced age of 27 she is not pretty, not rich, and in a society that treated penniless old maids as a burden on their family. She has a 'desire of an establishment' and knows that she cannot afford to turn down any offers of one. She settles down to a life of being bored by her husband and patronised by Lady Catherine in the vicarage in the village of Hunsford, keeping herself busy with her poultry (which are by implication more interesting than her husband). She represents the expectations for women at the time and Elizabeth's refusal to accept them. She understands Elizabeth better than she understands herself, knowing that 'her friend's dislike [of Darcy] would vanish, if she could suppose him to be in her power' thereby proving the extent to which Elizabeth is prejudiced. Another of her functions is to point out to the reader what could not be learned from Elizabeth because of the latter's blind spots, e.g. that Jane is likely to lose Bingley by being too passive, and that Darcy is in love with Elizabeth (p. 175).

Sir William Lucas

Charlotte's parents live unimaginatively and ostentatiously at Lucas Lodge. After his presentation at court and award of a knighthood Sir William was quick to give up his business and residence and move to Meryton, where he could lord it over the locals. He has given himself the airs of gentility but they are only skin deep, as he is an uncaring parent and tactless host whose only aim is to name-drop and show off; his desire to impress through grovelling is particularly noticeable on his visit to Rosings. His effect on the novel is to show that manners ('civilities') without morals are valueless, and the more effusive the style the more superficial and suspect the content. Had he continued working to acquire wealth as opposed to just status, he could have provided better for his children and Charlotte would not have had to sacrifice herself to the dreadful Mr Collins. Lady Lucas does not feature in her own right, which is itself indicative of her husband's dominance and talkativeness. He is not a sensitive or intelligent man, and in some ways could be seen as an older version of his son-in-law. Maria Lucas, Charlotte's younger sister, travels with her father to Hunsford and plays a quiet supporting role as the excuse for the visit.

Lady Catherine de Bourgh

Widow of Sir Lewis de Bourgh, of Rosings Park in Kent, Lady Catherine, as well as being a comic caricature (and model for Oscar Wilde's Lady Bracknell) is a plot device in attempting to prevent the union of Darcy and Elizabeth. She is an aristocrat, with the attendant characteristics of being opinionated, selfish and pretentious, which Austen could not abide and which are reflected in her unaccommodating Norman castle of a name. Darcy is her nephew through her deceased sister, Anne Fitzwilliam, having been married to Darcy's father. Her daughter, also Anne, has a 'sickly constitution' and lacks accomplishments, but she is the Rosings heir and, according to her mother, Darcy's intended bride to unite the two estates and keep everything in the family. Anne is a cipher in the novel, and cannot exert herself to speak, thus giving the impression that she has been crushed by her domineering mother. The said matriarch is the epitome of an **oxymoronic** 'dignified impertinence' and her pastime is 'dictating to others'. She interferes in the domestic arrangements of Hunsford and gives unsolicited advice to everyone she comes in contact with. Elizabeth describes her, even before meeting her, as 'arrogant' and 'conceited'; Wickham confirms that she is 'dictatorial and insolent'; Darcy is 'ashamed of his aunt's ill-breeding' (ironic given his views on Elizabeth's family), and Mr Collins attempts to recommend her as being 'all affability and condescension'. She is satirised for her *lèse-majesté* manner of treating her inferiors and, by implication, for her failures as a lady of the manor: '…whenever any of the cottagers were disposed to be quarrelsome, discontented or too poor, she sallied forth into the village to settle their differences, silence their complaints, and scold them into harmony and plenty.'

Colonel Fitzwilliam

The colonel, who is 'about thirty, not handsome, but in person and address most truly the gentleman', is the nephew of Lady Catherine and of her deceased sister Lady Anne, Darcy's mother, and therefore cousin to Darcy. As another army officer he provides a foil against which Wickham can be judged badly. His manners are 'much admired' and therefore he is also a contrast to his cousin, with whom he is co-guardian of Georgiana. He would like to propose to Elizabeth but cannot afford to. This complicates the plot and relationships, but paves the way for Darcy to continue to be interested in Elizabeth, since the colonel does not regard her family as an obstacle to her marrying well. He sets a good example in valuing someone for their own qualities and not their relatives; he also shows the constraints imposed on choice of partner by lack of income and the injustices inherent in being a younger son.

Georgiana Darcy

Aged 16, Darcy's sister is 'exceedingly shy' and not an appropriate match for Bingley. Her role is to be a victim of Wickham and an explanation of Darcy's hatred for him in his role as her protector. When Darcy tells Elizabeth he wishes to present his sister to her, we know that he must still have hopes of an alliance with her. Elizabeth recognises in Georgiana family traits that cast light on her brother's reserve and support his claim that he does not know what to say to strangers. As Elizabeth's sister-in-law she benefits from the latter's confidence and liveliness, showing the effects of a good influence.

Charles Bingley

Aged 22 and a resident of London, Bingley takes on a short lease as tenant of Netherfield Hall while he decides where to buy a permanent property with the wealth his father acquired in trade. He is the compliant friend of Darcy, whom he invites to join him there, along with his own two sisters and the elder sister's husband. The neighbourhood declares him to be 'amiable'. Elizabeth tellingly accuses Bingley of a 'want of proper resolution'. His weakness shows in his allowing Darcy to persuade him that Jane is not interested in him and to drop his acquaintance with her despite being attracted. A 'ductility of temper' is viewed as a fault in a novel that makes it clear that one should not give in 'without conviction'. He says proudly of himself (p. 42)

that 'Whatever I do is done in a hurry', exposing his lack of sense and reason. Darcy admits that Bingley has 'stronger dependence on my judgement than on his own', which is a serious lack of moral fibre and could have led to tragic consequences in a different genre of novel. He is not clever, unlike his friend, but is 'sensible, good humoured, lively' (p. 16) and makes a suitable partner for Jane.

Caroline Bingley

The younger of Charles's sisters, she fancies herself as Darcy's future wife. She mocks Elizabeth and criticises her family to make Elizabeth seem common in Darcy's eyes. Worth £20,000 a year, she looks down on the inhabitants and entertainments of Meryton, comparing country life unfavourably to town life and being generally superior. Her jealousy of Elizabeth ironically makes Darcy more not less interested in her rival by her drawing his attention to Elizabeth with her vicious comments. She is not a reader and is easily bored. Her treatment of Jane is cruel, in allowing her to believe that Bingley will marry Georgiana Darcy and in keeping Jane's presence in London a secret from her brother.

Louisa (Bingley) Hurst

The elder of Charles Bingley's morally ugly sisters also resides with him at Netherfield Hall, although she is married. Both sisters are described by Elizabeth as 'proud and conceited' and guilty of 'superciliousness', and they are only distinguished from each other by the elder sister saying and doing less, presumably since she does not need to compete to attract a husband. Since it is unthinkable that Jane and Elizabeth could ever fall out with each other, it is a damaging admission that Louisa and Caroline are in 'danger of hating each other' if they have to spend any time alone together.

Mr Hurst

We must presume him to be self-indulgent, since whenever he is present he is consuming, idling or sleeping, and he has no opinions on any subject. Gluttony and sloth are his deadly sins, and he is rarely seen standing up; 'he was an indolent man, who lived only to eat, drink and play at cards' (p. 35) and 'The latter was thinking only of his breakfast' are revealing and damaging narrator's comments. He provides a foil for Bingley, who is more lively, amiable and considerate than his brother-in-law, and for Darcy, who is much more abstemious, and a reader rather than a card player. His apparently loveless relationship with Mrs Hurst is an example of a bad marriage and a lesson in what should be avoided.

Mr and Mrs Gardiner

Edward Gardiner of Gracechurch Street, London, is the brother of Mrs Bennet. Elizabeth is not ashamed of her aunt and uncle, and appreciates her uncle being a

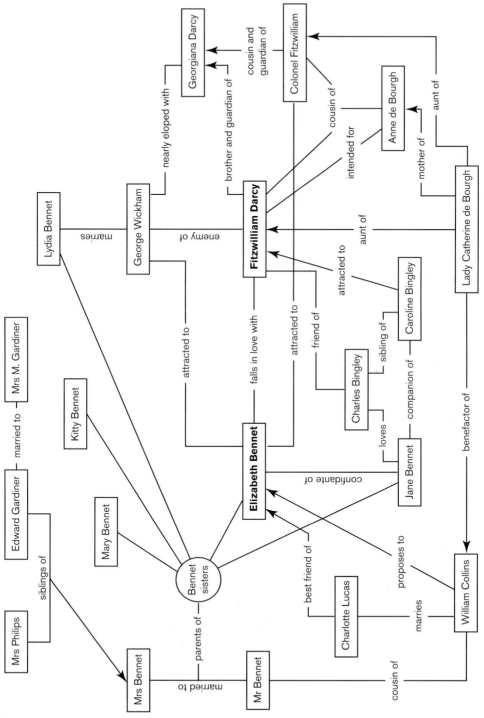

Character map

Source: http://upload.wikimedia.org/wikipedia/en/5/54/Pride_and_Prejudice_Character_map.png

'sensible, gentlemanlike man' who is 'well bred and agreeable', but his occupation in trade is considered insufficiently genteel by the Bingley sisters and Lady Catherine, and even Darcy agrees that it must lessen the chances of the Bennet sisters marrying well. The Gardiners have four young children, 'two girls of six and eight years old and two younger boys'. This is apparently so that the Gardiners' commitment to sorting out the mess in the Bennet family can be seen as all the more selfless when they have their own large family to support on their limited finances. The function of the Gardiners is a moral one, to show that one should judge by behaviour and not by wealth or its source. Mrs Gardiner is the voice of objective perception and reason in the novel, and gives Elizabeth good advice on several occasions, whilst also knowing when to keep silent. She understands Elizabeth's feelings for both Wickham and Darcy before Elizabeth herself does. Mr Gardiner takes on the paternal role abdicated by Mr Bennet: he continues to search for Lydia, and works together with Darcy to settle her position. Elizabeth values 'his intelligence, his taste, or his good manners'. They are better parents in every way than the Bennets, and in addition they have the important qualities of 'cheerfulness', 'affection and intelligence'.

Mr and Mrs Philips

Mr Philips is the attorney at Meryton, who married a Miss Gardiner, Mrs Bennet's sister. They are an excuse for Lydia to be constantly going off to Meryton to catch sight of and dine with the soldiers. Mrs Philips visits Longbourn to gossip with her sister. Her husband is described derogatorily as 'the broad-faced stuffy uncle Philips, breathing port wine'. Their role is to provide evidence for the reservations various characters have about belonging to or entering into a liaison by marriage with the Bennet family.

Character types

In this novel, characterisation is conveyed through narrative and dialogue, which are inseparable and mutually reinforcing, rather than through description. Austen fans always cite their enjoyment of her characters' credibility and individuality, which is achieved largely through their own speech, whereby they are presented as personae in a drama who independently reveal themselves through their utterances and how they relate to what the other characters have said just before, and which often gives a different impression from the one intended or assumed to have been conveyed.

Very few characters, of either gender, have a job or work to go to. They either visit and leave cards, sit in parlours, or take aimless walks. Meals are referred to but not actually eaten, clothes are discussed but not actually put on; everything seems to take place in the planning but not in the execution. The characters exist in dialogue but seem distant from their bodies and their functions, in the name of elegance and propriety; it is difficult to imagine an Austen character blowing their nose. As with the layout and decor of houses, personal appearance is ill-defined, yet characters' values are clearly exposed, the abstract always being more important than the concrete.

Romance character types

The traditional characteristics of romance and biblical stories are: love between the rich and powerful (usually male) and the poor and humble (usually female), quests and rescues, heroes and villains, dragons and fairies, extremes of temperament between siblings, absent or invalid mothers and distant or tyrannical fathers, headstrong and unheeding sons or daughters. These features became transmuted and more subtle over time, but they are still discernible in Austen's character types. For instance:

- Lady Catherine de Bourgh is the guardian dragon of the treasure; the masculine, bossy, widowed aunt.
- Fitzwilliam Darcy is the saviour knight in shining armour who overcomes his enemies and rescues damsels in distress.
- George Wickham is the charming villain who shamelessly deceives and seduces the ladies and exploits the men; a wolf in sheep's clothing.
- Mrs Bennet is the brainless, attention-seeking woman who attracted a husband with her looks and doesn't know when to stop talking.
- Mr Bennet is the cynical, irresponsible father who will do anything for the sake of peace and entertainment.
- Mary Bennet is the humourless, unattractive, tedious 'bluestocking' who lives her life second-hand through books but is not as clever as she thinks.
- Lydia Bennet is the self-indulgent, wayward, selfish girl who thinks she knows best and causes lots of trouble for everyone else.
- Charlotte Lucas is the plain, pragmatic girl who is second choice but achieves her goal through sheer determination.
- Caroline Bingley is the bitchy, jealous rival who will do anything to get her man.

Austen has been criticised for including only a narrow range of social types in her works. Her characters range in social status from minor aristocrats to commercial bourgeoisie and include substantial landowners, small landowners, lawyers, the clergy and servicemen. Though these all fall within the class known as the gentry, they offer a sufficient microcosm of humanity for her purposes. There is no need for comic yokels; servants; artists; doctors, or foreigners. The world of Austen characters consists mainly of families or couples living in rural surroundings, who receive occasional visits from relatives. The age range is also restricted, since the elderly and children below middle teenage are also generally excluded as named characters. The middle-level rural gentry are the staple of her novels (we see little of town life), not only because this is the world she knew, but because by creating a contained and homogenous social sample every gradation of speech and behaviour within it becomes significant and comparisons are inescapable. Deviance from conformity to acceptable standards cannot be explained away by differences of background if they have all shared it, and must therefore be attributed to lack of moral fibre and/or deficiencies of upbringing.

Simple and complex characters

Austen's characters can be divided into the simple and the complex. E. M. Forster called simple characters **'flat'**, meaning incapable of surprising the reader, or of doing so in a convincing way. Jane and Bingley are simple, and so is their love. They are both incapable of taking initiative, of being unamiable or of asserting their own views. Jane occasionally says something valid, e.g. about Darcy (p. 176), but only according to her unswerving commitment to being nice, not because she is exercising any discriminatory judgement. Lydia is simple in being so single-minded, and cannot be made to exercise restraint or show shame when she has failed to do so. Charlotte Lucas is essentially simple, since she reacts logically and predictably to her situation in life both before and after becoming Mrs Collins, and it is this very straightforwardness and placidity that Elizabeth finds frustrating. It is hard to see what makes them friends, though one did not have many candidates to choose from in a small country community in which peers and neighbours were inevitably thrown together. Charlotte's tedious father's function is to provide an example and warning against snobbery and sycophancy, and to be the cause of embarrassment in his insensitive attempt to get Darcy and Elizabeth to dance together. Lady Catherine and Mr Collins are comic caricatures representing pride. Mrs Bennet is the same at the end as she is at the beginning of the novel, having learned nothing from the experiences her family has been through. The Caroline Bingley the reader sees never falters in her unpleasantness to the Bennets and pursuit of Darcy, thus making her a flat character, though at least she has a distinctive persona, unlike her cipher of a sister. Mr Gardiner rises to the occasion in the saving of Lydia, but in a way entirely consistent with the reader's expectations.

Although Forster claimed that all Austen's characters were 'capable of rotundity', it could be argued that the simple characters in this novel are incapable of responding in an unpredictable way to anything. Even when they are the catalyst for events with a beneficial outcome, as Lady Catherine is, this is unintentional on their part, as they only care about themselves and cannot see themselves as others see them. Their function is to be silly so that they cause things to happen to the complex characters, who would never have got themselves into such a situation without them, e.g. Mrs Bennet's single-minded pursuit of Bingley causes her to send

Jane off to Netherfield to catch a cold and then leave her there, which sets in motion the extended opportunity for Elizabeth and Darcy to observe each other. They also provide a foil for the more developed and intelligent characters who shine by contrast, since they are capable of thinking and feeling on an entirely different plane, whether good or evil. An intricate character is aware of implications and capable of judgement and choice, even if they make the wrong one.

Wickham is not simple because he presents a different face to different people, is fully aware of how he appears to others, and of the impropriety of his behaviour, but he chooses to continue to misbehave for personal gain, relying on his ability to charm, persuade and ingratiate himself. He deliberately manipulates both Darcy and Elizabeth (and presumably Darcy's father before that) and is therefore guilty of active malice rather than the passive sin of ignorance. Mr Bennet has moments of self-realisation and self-judgement that show there is more to him than just a comic stereotype who takes nothing seriously, and he therefore counts as '**round**'. It is when the two types clash, as in the proposal of Collins to Elizabeth, when both the moral dimension and the humour of the novel become most acute.

Darcy's transformation

Some readers are uncomfortable about the apparent sudden change in Darcy's character between the two halves of the novel, from unamiable to amiable. Darcy conforms to the stereotype of the deep and taciturn Romantic hero and therefore perforce is silent and aloof much of the time, giving an impression of coldness. It could be said that the friendship of Darcy and Bingley never rings quite true, as they are so incompatible in interests and personality, and that Darcy's initial rudeness towards Elizabeth and damage to Jane's spirits can never be made up for in the reader's eyes. However, he has already started to appreciate Elizabeth before he leaves Netherfield, so the change in him is gradual rather than sudden, and it could be argued that he doesn't in fact change much at all, as he is still far from talkative, sociable or teasable even by the end. In any case Elizabeth changes too, and the point of their relationship is that they both have the power to change each other for the better, which is Austen's definition of a perfect coupling, one which includes education.

Because there is a passing of time and a physical distance between Elizabeth and Darcy between Chapters 18 and 30 and Chapters 36 and 43, it is reasonable that he should have had opportunity to reflect on and improve his attitude during the first separation and his manner during the second. (He has already progressed by Chapter 18 to the point of asking Elizabeth to dance with him, though he hates dancing). It is made clear that Elizabeth's rejection of him and the reasons she gives for it shock him deeply and for the first time in his life he has had to judge himself. Not getting his own way for once is a kind of epiphany for him, the equivalent of the near-death experience causing a radical change of lifestyle, which was a plot device beloved of novelists of this period (see Tom Bertram's redemption in *Mansfield Park*). In any case there has never been any suggestion that Darcy's morals are at fault, and we are told that he has always been popular on home ground. Jane has always stood up for him, which prepares us for the discovery of his goodness, and the testimony of the Pemberley housekeeper gives a consistent overview of his character since a child. He makes one big mistake, which is to warn Bingley against Jane, but learns from this and apologises for having misjudged the situation (and his desire to save his friend from having Mrs Bennet as a mother-in-law is, to be fair, perfectly understandable and possibly even acceptable). It is because he is at home and not among strangers when he meets Elizabeth that he can be his true self, and his pleasant behaviour to the Gardiners is explicable simply in that they are civilised people, and not the Bennets or the Philips.

Couples and siblings

It was a convention of romance and eighteenth-century literature to create pairs of characters, often siblings, who were either indistinguishably similar or complete opposites. Bingley reveals the greater intelligence and complexity of Darcy's mind, just as Jane does for Elizabeth. They are both foils for the main characters, and also a similar pair in being too undiscerning and amiable. Their existence allows for a double wedding to be planned within one family, a convention of comedy. Obviously Darcy and Wickham are presented as a hero/villain pairing, which has to be reversed. The Bennet parents are opposites in character but similar, though for different reasons, in their neglect of the proper upbringing of their family, each drawing attention to the dangers of excess and deficiency. Mrs Bennet and Lady Lucas are both typical matrons intent on catching men for their daughters, using devious means if necessary. Kitty is potentially another Lydia, saved at the last by their separation. Charlotte and Elizabeth are an opposite pair to be compared in their manner of responding to proposals. Mr Collins and Lady Catherine are the two comic villains who compete in odiousness and pomposity. Mrs Hurst and Miss Bingley are a pair of ugly sisters to Elizabeth's Cinderella. The comparisons inherent in the pairings reinforce conclusions about the necessity of right conduct and balanced temperaments, the damage that bad influence can inflict, the ironies of similarity within assumed difference, and the suitability of the match between the hero and heroine in their not having a similar partner, other than each other.

Places

For Austen, places usually meant houses; the events in her novels take place almost exclusively indoors. Houses reveal their owners not so much because they indicate social status, though they do, but because how they are managed exemplifies moral status. (In *Mansfield Park* Fanny Price's home in Portsmouth is described as cramped, squalid and noisy, with insufficient servants.) Austen is vague about the designs and amount of accommodation, however, since, as with people, the tendency is towards the delineation of the type rather than the particular, in order for them to be more representative.

The Bennet household

Longbourn is the name of both the house and the village in Hertfordshire of which the Bennets 'were the principal inhabitants'. It would not be possible to draw a plan of Longbourn (either house or village), although so much of the novel takes place there. However, we do know that it has a shrubbery 'hermitage', and that Mr Bennet has a library. Jane and Elizabeth have a bedroom each, and there is room to put up Mr Collins when he forces himself upon them for a visit, so that suggests probably six bedrooms. Mrs Bennet mentions a female servant called Hill. They have a coach and two horses, but the latter are sometimes lent out to a local farmer so transport is not always available to them (hence the excuse for Jane being stranded at Netherfield). Mr Collins is pleased to have a claim to the house, whose estate is worth £2,000 a year.

Village life

Some houses are bigger and more imposing than others, like Lucas Lodge, so distinctions of rank among the gentry are evident, as is rivalry. Mrs Bennet is particularly anxious to outdo the Lucases, which makes it all the more galling for her that it is Charlotte Lucas who 'wins' their cousin, Mr Collins, and the future entitlement to Longbourn, rather than one of her own daughters. She is able to feel superior at the end, however, when she acquires two sons-in-law better than that of Sir William and Lady Lucas.

The novel begins with the tidings that Netherfield Hall has been let at last. Village life revolves around the manor house and the comings and goings of its residents and visitors, and Lambton and Hunsford are shown to be just the same as Longbourn. The local community is dependent on the manor house for entertainment, the local tradesmen welcome the business, and there is the possibility of employment for domestic staff, so everyone is pleased when it is inhabited, provided that it is by a 'settled family'. When a regiment of soldiers, and therefore lots of eligible bachelors, is also stationed there and billeted in 'lodgings', it is an even more exciting prospect for the locals, especially mothers of daughters of marriageable age. The arrival of any newcomer in an area of quiet routine causes a huge flutter of excitement and speculation, since they are rare, and unattached men with means even rarer, given that the occasional clergyman or relative of a neighbouring family is usually without much money or property to boast of.

As everyone knows everyone, one of the main pastimes for the local women is gossip. When Mrs Long tells Mrs Bennet all about the letting of Netherfield by 'a

young man of large fortune from the North of England', she could only have received this information by hearsay. That gossip is usually inaccurate is proved in Chapter 3 when the word is that Bingley is bringing a party of 12 to the Assembly Room dance, when in fact there are only six. There is such a lack of things to do that visiting Meryton to look at the latest ribbons or to buy a pair of gloves at the haberdasher's is a major event. Even this outing is not possible in inclement weather, which determined whether or not one could venture out for a walk.

Significant locations

London

The London area had over a million inhabitants (the first city in Europe to do so), and was several times larger than any other city in Britain. Big cities, particularly London and the fashionable spa town of Bath, are the venue for decadence, shame, unkindness and unhappiness in all Austen novels, and associated with loose morals in both low life and high society. Austen wrote in a letter to Cassandra from London in 1796: 'Here I am once more in this Scene of Dissipation & vice, and I begin already to find my Morals corrupted.' She is obviously joking and exaggerating, but the reputation of the capital for encouraging immoral behaviour and being a bad example to the rest of the country is nonetheless made evident. Mr Bennet is forced to travel there to try to sort out Lydia's social suicide in running off there with Wickham but not being married to him. Darcy owns a house in London, as all wealthy country estate owners did as a practical necessity, but does not seem to choose to spend much time there. The Bingleys, however, return to the fashionable West End after abruptly leaving Netherfield and it is there that Jane suffers while they ignore her. London represents fashion, class war and snobbery, as the Bingley sisters accuse the Gardiners of living in Cheapside, a commercial area of the city (though they actually live further east in Gracechurch Street); exactly where one lived in London (down to which side of the street) was an important indicator of social status.

Brighton

Austen knew about the fashionable south-coast seaside resort of Brighton because her brother Henry was stationed there after becoming a militiaman on the outbreak of hostilities with France in February 1793. Notorious as a place for fashion and recreation, and associated with the licentious behaviour of the Prince Regent and his decadent coterie, it is an unwise trip to Brighton that brings about the opportunity and moral context for Lydia's downfall. The gathering of the militia in a temporary military camp in Brighton make it an unsuitable place for respectable young girls to be, especially if inadequately chaperoned. In a letter of 8 January 1799 to Cassandra, Austen wrote: 'I assure you that I dread the idea of going to Brighton as much as you do, but I am not without hopes that something may happen to prevent it.'

Rosings

This grand edifice is situated in Kent, another of the home counties, and is the residence of the widow, Lady Catherine de Bourgh, and her daughter Anne. At nearby Hunsford Mr Collins lives in the rectory with his newly acquired and recently impregnated wife, Charlotte. Being invited to dine at Rosings is the highest honour imaginable for the sycophantic vicar, and he enjoys showing off this patronising privilege to the rest of the Lucas family and Elizabeth when they visit. The furniture is showy and tasteless, and Elizabeth is oppressed by being there. The Lucas father and daughters feel privileged to be able to take tea at the great house at her ladyship's whim, but Elizabeth finds the set-up insultingly hierarchical and would prefer not to be invited to Rosings at all rather than to be treated so patronisingly. Rosings estate is fenced by palings, which form a barrier representing the social exclusivity their owner believes in. Elizabeth has to turn back because her shoes are not adequate for the symbolic 'white frost' which lies within. Darcy is loitering within a grove belonging to his aunt's estate, divided from Elizabeth's path by a gate, when he hands her his letter and disappears into the 'plantation'. This is therefore a symbolic point where social boundaries are being transgressed.

Hunsford

The vicarage is an adjunct to Rosings Park, physically and socially, but distinctly separated from it by palings, symbolising both the acolyte role of the incumbent vicar and his clearly defined inferior status. Charlotte has tried to make it homely, with her poultry, but her husband wants to show it off to visitors as a superior residence. The action takes place in the front room, which gives a view of the road and takes the form of the Collins couple being able to appreciate in advance when they are to receive a condescending visit from Lady Catherine or her daughter.

Derbyshire

Although not particularly far north geographically, it was distant enough from Hertfordshire in a time of limited travel to count as another country for Elizabeth, one where new vistas can be viewed and new perspectives gained on life in general, and hers in particular; this is what the scenic tour of the Peak District with the Gardiners enables Elizabeth to do. It has hills and lakes and open vistas different from Hertfordshire, offering Elizabeth literally new prospects and attractions. Despite having had to leave suddenly and reluctantly, she returns with her perception changed, the travel having broadened her mind to admit other possibilities and desires. The rugged terrain, very different from that of her home county of Hertfordshire, symbolises Romanticism and it is therefore appropriate that it is there that Elizabeth becomes truly acquainted with the longing of her heart, a need for escape and a desire for independence. That her Aunt Gardiner, the only other truly intelligent woman in the novel, is her enthusiastic companion and comes from

Derbyshire herself is an important endorsement of everything that happens there, in Darcy country and the nostalgic landscape of her maidenhood. Jane's letter recalls Elizabeth to a dissatisfying home life and the limitations of her family.

Pemberley

Elizabeth does not recognise the true Darcy until she has seen his house. Commentators claim that her remark to her sister about when she first knew she was in love with him must be teasing or ironic, which it obviously is on one level, but in fact it can also be taken straightforwardly to mean that the 'correlation between the moral and the material' (Eagleton), between him and his house, is the final proof she needs that Darcy is the perfect gentleman and the right one for her. When Lady Catherine asks whether 'the shades of Pemberley' are to be polluted by her being connected to the Darcy family, she makes it sound as though Elizabeth is the serpent about to destroy the Garden of Eden. The language is ridiculously bombastic, because classical and extreme, and the ridicule rebounds upon the speaker, but the point is still being made that Pemberley represents paradise. Darcy appears out of the ground like a *genius loci*, at one with his property, a genial host and an almost unrecognisably amiable entity; such is the power of place and the idea of home. Darcy is Pemberley, and Elizabeth yearns for both:

> It was a large, handsome, stone building, standing well on rising ground, and backed by a ridge of high woody hills; and in front, a stream of some natural importance was swelled into greater, but without any artificial appearance. Its banks were neither formal, nor falsely adorned. Elizabeth was delighted. She had never seen a place where nature had done more, or where natural beauty had been so little counteracted by an awkward taste. They were all of them warm in their admiration; and at that moment she felt that to be mistress of Pemberley might be something! (p. 235)

Uncomfortable in drawing rooms, Darcy can now be seen and appreciated in his natural surroundings and true element, in which he can talk about fishing. The interior of the house is also described in terms that could be applied to its owner: 'well-proportioned', 'handsome', 'real elegance'. The description of Pemberley is an example of the eighteenth-century tradition of 'moralized landscape design in which an appropriate balance of nature and art, beauty and its use is the sign of a properly responsible moral outlook' (Penguin edition notes p. 430). Not the apparel but the architecture, grounds and decor proclaim the man.

Plot and structure

A little action goes a long way in the prescriptive context of Austen's moral universe; the most seemingly minor incidents reveal serious defects of judgement and values: the world outside the drawing room is dangerous, card games are revealing, rudeness is the equivalent of rape, all physical contact is charged, and blushing has the force of sexual arousal (Darcy and Elizabeth mutually blush on p. 241). Darcy falls for Elizabeth after he notices she has muddied her petticoat, i.e. that she is daring and unconventional, thus do seemingly trivial events lead to major consequences in Austen's world.

The traditional dramatic device of a stranger arriving in town is the catalyst for various relationships and events to be set in motion. Starved of young men, the local community will compete to attract the attentions of the eligible bachelors about to arrive on the scene. The expectation is that they will not be single for long, and that as they are in so much demand, they are likely to have more than one admirer and a choice of future partners. Since sanctioned meetings can only occur at balls and in drawing rooms, this is where the plot developments occur. Nearly all of the events take place 'on stage', with the exception of Lydia's elopement and its aftermath in London. The reader goes where Elizabeth goes, so her visits to Kent, London and Derbyshire provide the movement of the novel.

The plot is generated by unforced character behaviour rather than by chance, which marks a new departure from the picaresque novels of the seventeenth and eighteenth centuries: Lydia's elopement; Mr Collins's proposal being refused by Elizabeth and accepted by Charlotte; Darcy's refusal to dance with Elizabeth at the Meryton Assembly; Lady Catherine's visit to Elizabeth. It is not easy to find an example of any event that is purely fortuitous, except Darcy arriving early at Pemberley while Elizabeth is still in the vicinity, but even this can be attributed to his efficiency in wanting to prepare in advance for his guests.

The plot of the novel takes just over a year, from early autumn 1811 to late autumn 1812.

Romance plots

The novel is in outline and outcome typical of all Romance plots and similar to, for instance, Shakespeare's *The Taming of the Shrew*, even down to the placid sister and the shrewish sister. A small close-knit community experiences an unexpected arrival of strangers to set the neighbourhood a-flutter, especially since they are men possibly in search of a wife and are the local women's only chance of meeting men and finding marriage partners when there is a shortage of suitable local candidates. Women must do the waiting while men do the travelling and proposing. In Romantic fiction it is always a new doctor (see *Cranford*), vicar or tenant who is the catalyst and dramatic focus, because his advent creates expectations, causes rivalries, and generally changes the nature of the pre-existing relationships. There is enmity between men who have previously quarrelled in each of the newly arrived groups, and the community is deceived into backing the wrong one; the real villain is revealed as a serial seducer and fortune-hunter, while the real hero performs a noble action in secret, to help his beloved, which becomes known to her. The pairs of lovers (and it is a feature of romance that there should be more than one) are separated by the machinations of others, and their own misunderstandings, but come together happily at the end, having defeated their ill-wishers and learnt from their mistakes.

Delaying tactic

As in Shakespearean opening scenes, we hear the main character discussed and disagreed over, being the favourite of one parent and not the other, before meeting her; this builds up expectation and interest, as does being told that 'Lizzy has something more of quickness than her sisters'. One of Jane's letters from London is delayed so that two arrive together in Derbyshire and Elizabeth and the reader can be put in the picture in one go about the events concerning Lydia, which actually took place over several days, with a cumulative effect of disaster. There is a delay in Mr Gardiner's letter reaching Longbourn to tell his brother-in-law that the situation has been resolved, which causes the anxiety to be prolonged. There is no reason for Bingley's delay in proposing, which requires him to visit Longbourn several times on his own, except in order to heighten the tension for the reader, the girls, and Mrs Bennet's nerves.

The title of the novel

The title of the novel comes from Fanny Burney's *Cecilia* (1782), at the end of which the phrase is used three times. Pride was the first and worst of the **seven deadly sins**, the one which caused Lucifer's fall in the book of Genesis and his transformation from the brightest and best of the angels into Satan, the king of Hell. As Mary Bennet opines, 'pride is a very common failing,' but vanity and pride are different things, though the words are often used synonymously. A person may be proud without being vain. Pride relates more to our opinion of ourselves, vanity to what we would have others think of us.

The original title of the novel was *First Impressions*, and was a warning not to judge, or pre-judge (the meaning of 'prejudice') too swiftly and superficially from first and therefore inevitably superficial impressions. Austen does not subscribe to the concept of love at first sight. It was an important moral doctrine at the time that choice, a word with spiritual connotations, should be based on fact and not rushed into because of habit, the authority of someone else, a partial (in both senses) view, purely sensory perceptions, or personal interest. First impressions are often unsound and delusory, are suspiciously close to being products of the imagination rather than of reason, and should always be resisted by a right-thinking and prudent person. The follies consequent upon deciding without the evidence of reflective experience are illustrated in different ways by Mrs Bennet and Mary, who each have either the reflection or the experience but not both.

Darcy and pride

In addition to Darcy, other characters in the novel are guilty of pride, i.e. of having an excessively high opinion of themselves or behaving with conceit, arrogance or disdain. Elizabeth calls it 'discernment' but this is just a form of pride. She has a high opinion of her wit and ability to amuse through being critical, which her father is also guilty of and encourages in her. Mary Bennet suffers from an unjustified complacency about her own abilities and 'was always impatient for display' (p. 25), though, according to her own definition, this is more vanity than pride. The Bingley sisters and Lady Catherine are other contenders, with their superiority complexes, and of course Mr Collins must be awarded a star prize, for although he appears obsequious, this does not detract from his real opinion of himself that he is supremely deserving and justifiably appreciated. He is in a 'state of angry pride' after being rejected by Elizabeth. In addition to it being a topic of conversation between major characters, many minor characters also bring up the subject of pride and vanity in the novel, such as Mr Collins, Charlotte Lucas, her brother and Mary Bennet, thereby making it a recurring **motif**. Nearly everyone is accused of it at some stage, even timid Georgiana Darcy (by Wickham).

Reserve can often be interpreted as pride — and Darcy's sister is also shy — but Darcy is in fact too proud in not minding or correcting the impression he gives of being proud. Mrs Bennet declares him to be 'high and conceited' and 'ate up with pride'. Even Kitty calls him a 'tall, proud man', and although we cannot trust their judgements they are saying what everyone else is also thinking. His comment on Elizabeth is disdainful and he doesn't take care that she shouldn't overhear him. The comment is itself a proud one: 'not handsome enough to tempt me' — as though he deserves better than anyone else. His not being willing to dance is also an anti-social stance for the time, and can be interpreted as being a criticism of those who do indulge in this pastime. He has a low opinion of Meryton and its parochial inhabitants. His being a man of few words lays him open to a charge of not thinking others worth the bother of talking to. He expects Elizabeth to not only accept his first lordly proposal but to be grateful for and overawed by it, because of his social rank. Marriage to one person meant 'connections' to many others, and he has too high an opinion of himself, having been spoilt from birth, to think it appropriate that either he, or anyone in his social circle, should become connected to the Bennet family. This belief, put into action in his advising Bingley to think no more of Jane, causes great pain to her, and to Elizabeth on her behalf. Elizabeth describes his letter explaining his actions as 'all pride and insolence'. This meddling in the affairs of others could well have damaged Bingley's future happiness also. In the end,

however, Elizabeth tells her father that Darcy has no 'improper pride', even though he himself has owned up to the fault.

Elizabeth and prejudice

In addition to Elizabeth, other characters in the novel are guilty of prejudice, i.e. a preconceived or irrational adverse judgement without examination of the facts of the particular case. Mrs Bennet has preconceived views on just about everything, and gossip and prejudice feed off each other. Mrs Gardiner is influenced by hearing that Darcy was 'formerly spoken of as a very proud, ill-natured boy', and is forced to change her opinion later after receiving the testimony of one who knows, his house-keeper. The inhabitants of Meryton decide after only one evening of distant exposure to Darcy that 'His character was decided. He was the proudest, most disagreeable man in the world'. Lady Catherine is prejudice personified, constantly proclaiming what is and what is not acceptable on every matter under the sun, including governesses and 'coming out'. Mr Collins has a view of women that borders on the insulting, and his misconceptions about them and lack of sympathy for them count as a prejudice towards the other sex. People in trade were looked down upon by the aristocracy and landed gentry, represented by the Bingley sisters, and Darcy has unquestioningly inherited this prejudice; he learns from meeting the Gardiners that some of them are, in fact, worthy of his respect. Though he is right to be prejudiced against Elizabeth's mother and her younger sisters, since they provide him with plenty of evidence of their failings, he initially lumps the two older sisters in with this blanket dismissal and has to learn to be more discriminating.

Elizabeth's prejudice against Darcy causes her to fall into the trap of being uncritical and credulous of Wickham, and thereby misjudging the characters of both of them, deceived, like many a Shakespeare character, by appearances. She says later of Darcy and Wickham respectively: 'One has got all the goodness, and the other all the appearance of it.' It is a sign of her increased maturity that she has learnt to recognise the difference. She is 'resolved against any sort of conversation' with Darcy at the Netherfield ball, since she is 'determined to hate' him, and has previously promised never to dance with him . She admits to Jane that she 'meant to be uncommonly clever in taking so decided a dislike to him without any reason', i.e. that she was governed by prejudice, and this is also the cause of her double standards in criticising Charlotte for marrying for money but thinking it acceptable that Wickham should do the same with Miss King. Her defect is to betray her own principles and 'wilfully to misunderstand everybody'; she is too quick to form opinions and, delighting in her own powers of perception, she employs her wit too readily and is often proved to have jumped to conclusions; even Jane is on several occasions nearer the mark in her explanations about other characters' behaviour. Wickham provides a support for the version of events she wishes to believe and therefore bolsters her misconception by appearing to lend it veracity and validity.

Ironically it is she who tells Darcy that he should not be blinded by prejudice and that it is incumbent upon him to be 'secure of judging properly at first' (p. 92).

Fortunately her trust in language finally saves her, as it is reading Darcy's letter, separated from his person, that convinces her that she has been mistaken about him, although she at first tries to block out his appeal by adopting 'a strong prejudice against every thing he might say' (p. 198). She then has her moment of **anagnorisis** when she recognises that she has been 'blind, partial, prejudiced, absurd'. She must do penance and suffer her punishment awhile, to emerge a chastened and better person. One cannot judge others if one knows not oneself, and this was the basis of tragedy. Elizabeth is reborn when she says: 'Till this moment I never knew myself.' At the end of the novel she tells Darcy 'how gradually all [my] former prejudices had been removed'. Because of her prejudice she very nearly loses the right man for her, and a fine house and future.

Themes

Themes are the fundamental and often universal ideas explored in a literary work. The opening chapter sets us the expectation that the story will be about courtship and marriage, and the financial and social considerations involved in the need to catch husbands for the girls are made clear from the outset. In addition to this general Austenian theme, and the specific ones to this novel of pride and prejudice, which are dealt with separately, there are other moral and abstract concepts that serve as themes in the novel.

Reason

A word used nearly 100 times in the novel in grammatical variants of 'reason' and 'rational', it is the fundamental, and Christian, precept that defines what it is to be human, and what divides the characters into distinct categories is whether they think or do not think. It was also an important topical issue following the publication of Mary Wollstonecraft's *Vindication of the Rights of Woman* (1792), which argued that women should be allowed to be credited with reason, and it is to this that Elizabeth is alluding when she tells Mr Collins that he should treat her as a 'rational creature speaking the truth from her heart' (p. 106). On p. 202 Elizabeth has a revelation that her sin had been to drive reason away and the rest of her mistakes automatically followed. It is used more and more as the novel progresses and as it becomes reinstated as the guiding principle. Elizabeth confesses in Chapter 40 that she took a dislike to Darcy 'without any reason', thus reducing herself to the level of her sisters ('In vain did Elizabeth attempt to make [Kitty] reasonable'). By the end she can tell Lady Catherine: 'I am not to be intimidated into anything so wholly unreasonable' (p. 337). Ironically this stance is interpreted by her **interlocutor** as proof

of her not being 'reasonable' (p. 339), and their verbal duel seems as much about who is the more rational as about a possible liaison between their families, since Elizabeth says, presumably sarcastically, that Lady Catherine's journey to Longbourn from Rosings to break off the supposed engagement 'was a rational scheme to be sure!' Darcy has reasons for everything he does, whereas all the other characters (except the insignificant Mr Gardiner) fail in this area by either not having any or by faulty rationalising. Even Mrs Gardiner, a sound thinker in many ways, is irrational in her belief that Wickham must be a nice young man because he comes from Derbyshire (her former home) and she initially condemns Darcy from hearsay as having been 'a very proud, ill-natured boy' (p. 141).

Reason is what must prevail for a work to be defined as a comedy ('Life is a comedy to those that think, a tragedy to those that feel'), as pointed out by Elizabeth's comment on the engagement of Jane and Bingley: 'the happiest, wisest, most reasonable end!' (p. 328). Reflecting back at the end of the novel, 'How earnestly did she then wish that her former opinions had been more reasonable' (p. 355), she then teases Darcy with the idea that it was 'perfectly reasonable' of him to fall in love with her because she was different from other women and he was 'sick of civility, of deference, of officious attention' (p. 359). On the next page the dialogue continues to talk about what is 'reasonable'. Because different characters use *reason* to mean an accordance with their own wishes, it is a slippery word to define and often used ironically, e.g. Mrs Bennet thinks Elizabeth needs to be 'brought to reason' for not accepting Mr Collins's proposal (p. 108).

Judgement

This is a moral imperative of biblical proportions, and the one that underpins the novel; pride and prejudice are lapses of judgement; until they know and can judge themselves, which is the journey Elizabeth and Darcy have to make, they make erroneous judgements of each other's beliefs and behaviour. The reader in turn must exercise judgement on the characters, and to make this more challenging, the narrative viewpoint can often not be trusted, so that we can make the same mistakes as Elizabeth does, and the novel serves as a kind of *Pilgrim's Progress* test of our own moral status. The lively characters of Lydia and Wickham are the dangerous ones we should not be taken in by, but which we might be tempted to find attractive, especially in comparison to those who are staid or insipid. Mrs Bennet's inability to exercise judgement is mocked, although she cannot help her 'mean understanding'. The recognition of pretence and illusion is part of having judgement; if there is deception then the truth is being hidden, and it is a Christian duty to uncover truth and act upon it.

Upbringing

Mary Lascelles said: 'Faulty upbringing was a favourite theme in an age when many novels were written by, for and about women: mothers must be foolish, absent or dead; fathers or guardians eccentric' (Dent introduction to *Emma*). Orphans are a feature of romance literature, since they are unprotected children vulnerable to danger and jealousy (represented by wild beasts and plotting stepmothers in fairy tales) and this creates tension, drama and pathos. The Bennet sisters are quasi-orphans, having a pair of inadequate and neglectful parents, so they are at risk of falling into error and of becoming social victims. Lydia 'has never been taught to think on serious subjects' and 'has been allowed […] to adopt any opinions that came in her way (p. 269). The outcome of one's upbringing was believed to be a mixture of natural disposition and guidance, the latter considered more influential than formal education. Poor family role models are to blame for most errant behaviour in Austen. Mr Collins was brought up by 'an illiterate and miserly father' (p. 69); Darcy was more fortunate in having been 'taught what was right' and 'given good principles' as a child, but his failings stem from not being taught to correct his temper, being spoilt for many years as an only child, and allowed to develop 'pride and conceit', until cured by Elizabeth.

Moderation

Aristotle's precept of moderation in all things is the definition of decorum. Austen supported the Augustan tenet of restraint and was deeply wary of the forms of excess and self-indulgence that later characterised the Romantic movement. In particular she believed that moderation in speech and feelings were required for polite society to function without vulgarity and embarrassment. Deficiency is also a failure of moderation and is criticised in the guise of Mr and Mrs Bennet and, though more gently, in Jane and Bingley; being too pliant and amiable shows a want of discernment and independence. Lydia and her mother know no moderation of feeling or expression, or in the pursuit of their goals; Mrs Bennet is either downcast to the point of taking to her bed or uncontainedly delighted. Mr Collins also represents excess in the novel; he talks for too long and overwhelms people, such as Mrs Philips who is 'awed by such an excess of good breeding' (p. 72), a contradiction in terms.

Balance

The marriage of Elizabeth and Darcy is a reconciling of energy and reason: the rambling and playful versus the rigid and regulated; significantly, 'uniting them' are the last two words of the novel. Balance is needed in human temperament too: Mr Collins originally had 'great humility of manner' but has gone to the other extreme of being conceited, and is now 'an oddity' who is a contradictory 'mixture of pride and obsequiousness'. Comedy is predicated upon the concept of harmony by means of the eradication of extremes. The energetic individual in need of space must be contained within the boundaries of society and therefore his or her excesses must be repressed, or at least rechannelled into love; Romantic open spaces and unbounded liberty must be circumscribed by the classical walls and limits of form.

Manners

Although good manners are the hallmark of civility, unlike morals they can be counterfeited. Sir William Lucas and Wickham have notably courteous manners but these hide their moral weaknesses (vanity and fecklessness) and an abdication of responsibility towards their professions and acquaintances, the latter more seriously than the former because more deliberate in and conscious of his speech and actions. Those who talk only of their own interests are, by definition, bad-mannered. Mr Collins likes to think he has good manners, but they are an affectation and overdone. He pays no regard to his interlocutors and causes them frustration and embarrassment — with the exception of Lady Catherine, who accepts his fawning as nothing less than her due.

Gratitude

This is another Romance theme, which takes the form in fairy tales of someone being awarded three wishes as reward for a service or punished for not being sufficiently appreciative of one. As humans should be grateful to their divine creator and benefactor, Wickham owes gratitude to Darcy and his family for the support he received from the latter's father, and conversely it is shocking to Elizabeth that Darcy has allegedly shown ingratitude to the son of the man his father admitted 'the greatest obligations' to. However, Collins's gratitude towards Lady Catherine is in excess of the facts of the case and invites mockery of both of them for the falsity of the relationship. Gratitude was automatically owed to parents, and Jane and Elizabeth carry out their filial obligations, though with difficulty in the latter's case, but the more to her credit because she finds it so. Mr Gardiner is an important focus for gratitude for his having 'readily promised every assistance in his power' to support his sister's family through its crisis, and it is telling that Mr Bennet, Elizabeth and Jane understand their obligation to their uncle, but Mrs Bennet is insufficiently appreciative. A bond of gratitude between the leading couple is mutual: Elizabeth's gratitude to Darcy for his efforts on Lydia's behalf, as well as her 'Gratitude, not merely for having once loved her, but for loving her still' (p. 253); his to her for having been 'taught a lesson [...] most advantageous', 'What do I not owe you!' (p. 349).

Improvement

Austen's heroines are required to select and finally acknowledge a beloved with whom they can undergo a process of mutual improvement. A suitable marriage is one of intelligent love where the partners can educate each other by offering the other what they are lacking in order to become Platonically complete: '...by her ease and liveliness, his mind might have been softened, his manners improved, and from his judgment, information, and knowledge of the world, she must have received benefit of greater importance' (p. 295). One is improved through lessons and reflecting on and learning from them. Darcy tells Elizabeth: 'You taught me a lesson

[...] By you, I was properly humbled' (p. 349). His letter teaches Elizabeth a lesson about the dangers of prejudice by revealing how she was fooled by Wickham. Kitty is young enough to be able to undergo 'improvement' when removed from Lydia's influence; under the guidance of her elder sisters she becomes 'less irritable, less ignorant, and less insipid'. Georgiana is improved by exposure to her new sister-in-law and her 'lively, sportive manner'; 'by Elizabeth's instructions' her 'mind received knowledge which had never before fallen in her way' and she starts to comprehend a world and relationships beyond her sheltered family life.

Images and symbols

In addition to reinforcing themes, imagery gives atmosphere, pattern, integrity and meaning to a text, and can help to delineate character. **Symbols** represent an abstract concept greater than themselves.

Eyes/view

Words pertaining to vision, in both physical and metaphorical senses, form an image cluster in the novel. Seeing and being seen was an essential part of the life of the actual and moral life of the times. It is also part of the novel's narrative approach to play ironically with viewpoint, and this image is related to the themes of judgement (judging by appearances, i.e. through the eyes) and prejudice, i.e. a **flawed lens** or a partial view. Elizabeth's bright eyes are her most compelling feature — the one which wins over Darcy — and reflect her spirit and intelligence. 'View' is used to mean prospect and outlook, applied both to the countryside and houses, as well as attitude and judgement. The two meanings are connected to the imagery of eyes and reflection, itself an ambiguous word, and these all come together in the context of Elizabeth's visit to Pemberley and the views and visions she is subjected to there.

Picture

In a pre-photographic world a picture meant a portrait or landscape painting, when this was the only way of creating a likeness. It is also used as an idiom to mean forming an impression of a character, as in the dialogue between Elizabeth and Darcy: "'...I could wish, Miss Bennet, that you were not to sketch my character at the present moment, as there is reason to fear that the performance would reflect no credit on either." "But if I do not take your likeness now, I may never have another opportunity"' (p. 92). Elizabeth falls in love with Darcy's picture on the wall at Pemberley, as well as with his likeness to the well-cultivated and aesthetically tasteful estate that belongs to him and therefore reflects him. To look as pretty as a picture was an ideal of the period, on the basis of which all costume and activity was predicated; everything must look attractive and posed, as in the movements and symmetry of the style of dancing; this is why Elizabeth's muddy petticoat is regarded as such a social faux pas by the Bingley sisters, who care only about appearances and superficialities, and why everyone is taken in by the picturesque Wickham in his colourful (but dangerous) coats.

Scheme

A much-used word in the novel, carrying more menace then than it does now. The original schemer was Satan — plotting first against God and then Adam and Eve in the Garden of Eden — and so, like the word 'evil' itself, it is forceful in the context of an author who rarely used strong language of any kind and regarded it as an impropriety in her characters to do so. A schemer is neither frank, open, honourable, trustworthy nor possesses any other of the gentlemanly virtues. Caroline Bingley schemes against Elizabeth and Jane in her pursuit of Darcy; Wickham schemes to marry a woman with money; Lydia plots the 'delicious scheme' (p. 212) of going off to Brighton; Mr Collins arrives at Longbourn with a scheme to marry one of the Bennet daughters; Lady Catherine's impromptu visit to Longbourn is a 'scheme'. No schemer is successful or to be admired in Austen, as by definition a scheme involves secrecy and manipulation of others. The only time Elizabeth schemes is in joining in her mother's plan to cause Jane to be stranded at Netherfield, and she is punished by the potential death of her beloved sister, who is incapable of scheming herself.

Performance

'The power of doing anything with quickness is always prized much by the possessor, and often without any attention to the imperfection of the performance' pp. 47–48). Simply being in public demands a performance, and most of the time Austen's characters are being watched, not just when dancing, singing, playing an instrument or a game, but when sitting, walking, talking and in every aspect of their daily lives conducted in public. Their parlours are the stage for the entrances and exits for the multitude of daily visitors, and their costumes are carefully designed with the aim of cutting a fine figure (and Caroline Bingley walks around the room as a performance for Darcy to appreciate hers). Their conversations were also planned and even rehearsed, and not only by Mr Collins; Mr Bennet and Mary deliver all of their utterances as bons mots to be appreciated by their audiences. Austen is suspicious of performers who are too adept at acting convincingly (like Wickham) or have a self-dramatising theatrical tendency (like Mrs Bennet), as neither can be presumed to be capable of genuine feeling. The word, however, disappears from the novel after Elizabeth has read Darcy's letter and they are no longer playing a part and hiding behind a mask.

Symbolic events and places

Balls are *par excellence* social gatherings for enjoyment, so when Elizabeth receives a snub at the Meryton assembly it has the shock factor of at least a slap across the face, because the disappointment she experiences is in a context of pleasure for everyone else, especially Jane. We realise that Darcy needs some refining of his manners because he does not care whether or not Elizabeth can hear him. Elizabeth arriving at Netherfield with mud on her petticoat is a symbolic moment in the novel, revealing and representing far more than itself. It shows the superficiality of the etiquette of the Bingley sisters, who are not truly refined or they would not embarrass a guest by drawing attention to her condition, and at the same time the genuine affection of Elizabeth for her sister in being brave enough to undertake a journey on foot and in the rain, no ordinary matter in those days and likely to result in more damage to the health than a soiled undergarment. To Darcy it symbolises that she is a passionate woman with a beating heart, and different from the doll-like creatures he is surrounded by, and his interest is sparked by this dramatic entry.

The main symbol in the novel is Pemberley, which reflects its owner, revealing the hidden and worthy side of his character and how those who really know him feel about him, and the importance to England of tradition and history and country life.

Humour, satire and wit

As well as fulfilling the generic definition of comedy by ending satisfactorily, Austen's novel is comic in the sense of containing humorous dialogue and amusing comments by the narrator and **authorial voice**. The humour is not only to amuse but is also a weapon for character assassination and a means of raising serious concerns about behaviour and the suitability of relationships.

One of the ways of creating humour is to clash simple with complex characters. In each case there is a marked difference in speech styles between the pairs of characters, and one character is allowed to be humorous at the expense of the other, who is made to look more insensitive and more foolish by the comparison:

– **Mrs Bennet and Mr Bennet:**
  she is made to seem ridiculous and he is made to seem witty; the marriage is made to seem an incompatible one.
– **Elizabeth and Mr Collins:**
  she seems to be striking a blow for feminism in being both more intelligent and rational than him and with a more enlightened view of relationships and marriage; he is made to look a fool for proposing to someone so unsuited to his wifely requirements and for continuing to pursue his case long after she has made her rejection clear.
– **Elizabeth and Lady Catherine:**
  the humour is ironic and contained in the certainty of the older woman and the refusal to be cowed of the younger, so that the battle's outcome is a reverse of normal expectations and those of Lady Catherine; her discomfiture is a come-

uppance that the reader must enjoy, having endured so much of her previous pontificating.

Comic devices

Austen uses a narrow range of humorous devices compared to some comic writers, since she rules out visual comedy completely; she relies on caricature, witticisms, **epigrams** and the situational comedy device of bringing together characters of different intellect, class, gender or agenda to generate amusement and misunderstanding. There are many examples of these even within the Bennet family conversations, and even Mr Bennet the ironist is caught out by the irony that Elizabeth now loves Darcy instead of hating him. In addition to Mr Collins and Lady Catherine, Sir William Lucas is also a caricature in that he manages to get in references to being presented at court whenever possible — or seemingly impossible — and Lydia is dangerously close to being one because of the limitations of the content of her utterances, which rarely stray beyond soldiers, clothing and having a laugh. There is comedy in the use of bathetic juxtapositions by the narrator or heroine, as in the inference that the arrival of Lady Catherine can be compared to a pig getting into the garden, and that the time taken to stir a fire is the amount of time needed for a change of mind about whom one should marry. The ironic viewpoint of Elizabeth is used as an intermittent comic device throughout the novel, to which Mr Bennet adds during his cameo appearances.

Satire

Elizabeth is a satirist who owns up to laughing at the follies and vices of her acquaintances. Irony draws attention to folly, but satire goes further in being a deliberate scathing attack with the aim of exposing to ridicule and contempt a type or an institution, and pointing out the damage they cause to others. The targets for the novel's satire are the clergy (Mr Collins); the aristocracy (Lady Catherine de Bourgh); social climbers (Sir William Lucas); irrational mothers (Mrs Bennet); negligent fathers (Mr Bennet). Jane and Bingley are gently mocked for their naivety, but they do not earn Elizabeth's or the reader's contempt. What distinguishes vice from folly is that it hurts others and is deliberate; Mrs Bennet is not educated, but Mr Collins is, and so is George Wickham, and they should know better.

Witty characters

Austen claimed in a letter to her niece (18 November 1814) that 'Wisdom is better than wit, and in the long run will certainly have the laugh on her side', though her readers would disagree, since they read her for her wit rather than her wisdom. Elizabeth is actually punished for her wit and has learned the need to curb it by the end of the novel. Darcy does not suffer from this affliction so will be able to help her to hold it in check. Mr Bennet is the most guilty of employing wit, practised at the expense of his wife, silly daughters and cousin, but he is punished, at least briefly, by his conscience and the necessary intervention of others to act on his behalf to sort out his youngest daughter's predicament. Although he does not much suffer much from this humiliation, and is unlikely to learn from it, Elizabeth makes it clear that he is seriously at fault, and while the reader is amused by him, he is not to be admired. The fact that Mr Bennet finds Wickham amusing is a black mark against his own judgement, which is based on wrong priorities. On the other hand, those who are incapable of supplying or appreciating wit, as a form of verbal dexterity, are presented as tedious; as usual the ideal is a balance. The important thing (and the lesson Elizabeth has to learn) is knowing when wit is and is not appropriate, and being capable of being serious about serious subjects.

Serious humour

Because this is a didactic novel, even the most humorous passages have a serious message. The different layers of narrative in the novel create complex ironies, verbal and situational, which have a comic effect but which also make serious moral statements.

Mr and Mrs Bennet's conversation in the opening chapter

This amusing dialogue reveals the temperamental and intellectual incompatibility between the parents which immediately forbodes the discovery of the faulty upbringing of their offspring, as well as highlighting the issues of what makes a good or bad choice of partner. Mrs Bennet's desperation to get her daughters married draws attention to the financial and property demands on young women and their parents and the undesirability of having that number of daughters, who need to be disposed of. We can immediately see the potential for Mrs Bennet being a cause of embarrassment and for Mr Bennet being neglectful of his responsibilities.

Mr Collins's proposal to Elizabeth (Chapter 19)

Although hilarious, there are many serious underlying points being made about the position of young women: their marriageability or otherwise; the injustice of entailed estates; their captive position in having to suffer such approaches; their duty to their parents and not to their own feelings; the myth that women say 'no' when they mean 'yes'. Elizabeth is actually taking a huge risk in turning him down, at the age of 20 and with no money to speak of — as Collins tactlessly reminds her — and knowing that her mother, at least, will be furious with her. This evokes our admiration for her independent spirit.

Dinner at Rosings (Chapter 29)

The laughable inquisition Lady Catherine subjects her guests to, her dominance in prying, interrupting and lecturing, and the discomfort she causes, all break the rules of true hospitality. She is an odious figure and does not deserve her station in society, which she abuses. Her manners are actually worse than those of the Gardiners, whom she despises as inferior, and therefore Austen is making the point that the social hierarchy is fortuitous, not meritorious, and ironically reversible.

Elizabeth's teasing of Jane (Chapter 59)

Elizabeth tells Jane that she fell in love with Darcy 'from my first seeing his beautiful grounds at Pemberley' (p. 353). This shockingly mercenary admission that she wants to be mistress of Pemberley can be dismissed as just teasing of her literal-minded sister. However, she is not only joking and mocking herself, she is condemning the materialism involved in the choice of marriage partners generally, and also showing an understanding of the connection between houses and their owners which is deeply significant and was, in fact, the reason for her allowing herself to fall in love with Darcy, despite the dangers of first impressions; people may deceive, but houses don't.

Letters

There are 21 letters printed in full in *Pride and Prejudice*, a novel that was originally in epistolary form (as was *Sense and Sensibility*), and in total there are 44 letters referred to.

Letters were the only form of communication at the time so that characters, and readers, are dependent on them for information (see p. 281). The letters in the novel serve all possible purposes in establishing or developing character, plot, theme and style, though their main function is to keep the reader informed of events occurring other than where Elizabeth is, i.e. in London and Brighton. Because the sisters and couples are frequently apart, letters are a vital link between them. However, these are not the only exchanges, and Elizabeth is not a particularly active letter writer, since it is the character, attitudes and behaviour of others that need to be revealed rather than hers, which the reader is already fully aware of.

As the voice and actual words of the character they function as **monologues** and give opportunities for the extended conveyance of attitudes and feelings which could not otherwise be revealed in a social context where conversation could not be so frank or one-sided. The style of a letter betrays the writer as much as the content, whether by revealing reserve or over-familiarity, sense or insensitivity; for instance, Mr Collins's lack of humanity is apparent in both his sentiments and their cruel expression. They are also the means of providing comedy or creating tension.

The letters in the novel

Chapter 7: Caroline Bingley to Jane, inviting her to come to Netherfield.
Chapter 7: Jane to Elizabeth, reporting her illness.

Chapter 13: Mr Collins to Mr Bennet, proposing to visit Longbourn.

Chapter 21: Caroline Bingley to Jane, informing her that the Netherfield party have all gone to London.

Chapter 26: Jane in London to Elizabeth, before seeing Caroline Bingley.

Chapter 26: Jane in London to Elizabeth, after seeing Caroline Bingley.

Chapter 26: Jane in London to Elizabeth, admitting Caroline Bingley's perfidy.

Chapter 35: Darcy's letter to Elizabeth (hand-delivered at Rosings), explaining his conduct.

Chapter 46: Jane's misdirected letter to Elizabeth at Lambton, breaking the news of Lydia's elopement.

Chapter 46: Jane's second letter to Elizabeth at Lambton, with new fears about Lydia.

Chapter 47: Lydia to Mrs Forster, announcing the elopement.

Chapter 48: Mr Gardiner in London to Mrs Gardiner at Longbourn, about inquiries after Lydia and Wickham.

Chapter 48: Mr Collins to Mr Bennet (opened by Jane), offering condolences to the Bennets about Lydia.

Chapter 49: Mr Gardiner to Mr Bennet, announcing the settlement of negotiations with Wickham.

Chapter 50: Mr Gardiner to Mr Bennet, containing further particulars of Wickham's affairs.

Chapter 51: Elizabeth to Mrs Gardiner, inquiring why Darcy was at Lydia's wedding.

Chapter 52: Mrs Gardiner to Elizabeth, giving the real story behind Lydia's marriage.

Chapter 57: Mr Collins to Mr Bennet, advising against an Elizabeth–Darcy match.

Chapter 60: Elizabeth to Mrs Gardiner, allowing her to indulge her imagination.

Chapter 60: Mr Bennet to Mr Collins, troubling him for congratulations.

Chapter 61: Mrs Wickham to Mrs Darcy, Lydia begging from Elizabeth on behalf of Wickham.

Function of the letters

A surprising number of characters write or receive letters in the novel. Some are informative (like those of Mr and Mrs Gardiner), but others are to interfere, demand or gloat (Mr Collins, Lydia, Mr Bennet), so that the purpose in writing reveals character type distinctly. The epistolary styles of Jane and Lydia, Mr Collins and Darcy, could not be more different and therefore serve to distinguish admirable from reprehensible characters. Most of the letters are in the second half of the novel, crossing physical divides and bridging gaps in knowledge and understanding, thus leading to the restitution of the two romantic relationships. The biggest flurry of letters is caused by Lydia's misbehaviour, which implicates and draws in the extended

Bennet and Darcy families, and both jeopardises and cements the relationship between Elizabeth and Darcy. Men were less commonly letter writers than women so it makes the situation of the elopement the more serious that the letters at this point are between father and uncle; they are practical and not social missives. Mrs Bennet, ever useless, never puts pen to paper, and her husband only to amuse himself.

Though some letters simply reinforce what we already know about the writer's personality, such as Jane's letters to Elizabeth (Chapter 26), Lydia's to Mrs Forster (Chapter 47) and Mr Collins's to Mr Bennet (Chapter 48), Darcy's letter to Elizabeth is crucial in allowing the reader — and its recipient — to become aware of a different character hidden beneath his social facade. Some critics maintain that Darcy's letter is unrealistic, contending that such a proud and reserved man would never reveal so many details of his private life. According to this view, the letter functions primarily as an artificial device through which Austen is able to introduce a large quantity of information while vindicating Darcy. One can argue, however, that the 'dreadful bitterness of spirit' in which Darcy claims to have written the letter explains its uncharacteristic nature. Regardless of how convincing it is, the letter serves its purpose: it reveals the truth about Wickham's relationship to Darcy and consequently shifts sympathy from the former to the latter. It is interesting to note that the idea of a man eloping with a young woman was already clichéd in the literature of Austen's era; nevertheless, its appearance in *Pride and Prejudice* serves a vital function, as it later provides Darcy with a motive (besides his love of Elizabeth) for helping Lydia after she elopes with Wickham.

Narrative modes

Austen's range and command of narrative modes is what enables her to create the dramatic and comic effects so appreciated by her fans. 'It is the continual diversification of the surface, the sparkling slightly effervescent quality of the narrative, that gives Austen's work its special flavour' (Hough). There are nine distinct narrative modes in her novels, and sometimes they merge into each other to convey even more complex effects. There are 26 speaking characters in *Pride and Prejudice*, almost twice as many as in *Sense and Sensibility*, but they all have a recognisable and distinctive voice or **idiolect**. Because so much of the novel is in dialogue, most of which consists of sparring between two parties, the novel is dramatic and has therefore attracted film makers. The latter half of the novel, however, is more interiorised as Elizabeth's consciousness.

1   Authorial voice

Often ironic, this differs from the narrative voice in being usually reflective and addressed directly to the reader. It is little used compared to other narrative modes, but memorable when it is. The opening sentence of the novel is clearly an opinion rather than objective narrative, and one that sets the tone for the novel. Though this first chapter is essentially for scene and character setting, it is done with a very light touch that avoids obvious and direct descriptive passages. The first sentence, an **aphorism** that sounds like the beginning of a Dr Johnson essay for the *Rambler*, seems to be a mockery of the stereotype of mothers of daughters in general and of Mrs Bennet in particular. With hindsight it becomes doubly ironic as the cliché is in fact shown to be a 'universal truth' by the subsequent marriage of her three daughters by the end of the novel, and she is proved right in thinking that Mr Bingley was in search of a wife.

The authorial voice is always obtrusive and occasionally clumsy: on p. 145, when the lack of subtlety of 'The letter which she wrote on this occasion to her sister, will prove what she felt' draws attention to the fictional construct; on p. 154, when the apparently throwaway word 'probably' jars as an abdication from the **omniscient narration** and an abrupt transition into Elizabeth's viewpoint; on p. 231, when there is what sounds like dismissiveness in the tone of 'It is not the object of this work to give a description of Derbyshire'; on p. 346, where there is an opting out of authorial responsibility with the bored comment — and one which breaks the illusion of realism — that Darcy 'expressed himself on the occasion as sensibly and warmly as a man violently in love can be supposed to do'; at the beginning of the final chapter where an authorial 'I' intrudes in 'I wish I could say...'; on p. 240 where the sudden rhetorical question 'What praise is more valuable than the praise of an intelligent servant?' stands out — this paragraph is a good example of where it is impossible to differentiate between Elizabeth's, the narrator's and the authorial voice.

Mr Bennet's mode is, like that of the author, ironic and epigrammatic, e.g. 'In such cases, a woman has not often much beauty to think of', which is what endears him to the reader, but misleads us into thinking that he has the author's approval. Elizabeth has inherited his ironic view of life and style of speech, which is what endears her to the reader, but misleads her into thinking that it is a sound basis for judgement.

2 Objective narrative

This voice is used to set the scene, explain the circumstances and introduce characters. It is a literary convention that we always believe factual information and statements made by the narrative voice (or we did until postmodernism). We have made a contract to be told a story and we trust the teller of it, and only notice that there is a narrative voice when it slips up, for example when Austen refers to Catherine by her full name and as Kitty in consecutive sentences on p. 326. However, Austen inserts value judgements and opinions of characters as well as facts into this apparently objective mode, which means we must not be 'dull Elves' and have to use our ingenuity to be aware of when this is happening and guard against

being misled. There is an ironic reference to Mrs Bennet as 'his lady' on the first page that is clearly not simply a factual label for the unladylike wife of Mr Bennet, though it purports to be so. There are passages, such as the long paragraph on page 17, which begin as objective narrative but which seamlessly slide into authorial voice; we are told that the Bingley sisters 'were in the habit of spending more than they ought, and of associating with people of rank; and were therefore in every respect entitled to think well of themselves, and meanly of others'. The beginning of this quotation is factual but the word 'therefore' signals the ironic comment to come. Nearly all of the final chapter, summing up the future for each of the main characters, is delivered in the narrative voice. It is also used to tell us things that Elizabeth cannot know, such as Charlotte's 'scheme' to win Mr Collins for herself by setting out to meet him 'accidentally' on page 119.

When relationships have been resolved Austen tends to replace speech with objective narrative; or when she wishes to economise the narrative by summarising or compressing part of a dialogue. On page 185, for instance, Darcy begins in direct speech, and dialogue ensues on the following page, but the rest of the previous page is in a mixture of reported speech and objective narrative. The delaying of Elizabeth's reply builds up tension, as does the description of her increasing exasperation.

3 Coloured narrative

Some of the narrative is delivered directly by Elizabeth, unmediated by the narrative voice. This is necessary to enable the reader to be deceived, along with the heroine, about matters that will be revealed later to have been fallacious. This creates dramatic effect and enables there to be a **denouement**, but it also has a moral purpose in showing the reader, rather than just telling us, how easy it is to be taken in by someone we like and think we can trust. This mode is used by Austen more than objective narrative, although Elizabeth does not overshadow the novel in the way Emma does with her views; Darcy, Mr Bennet, Jane, Bingley, the Gardiners, and Mrs Reynolds must all be agreed with by the reader at times. However, this mode demands provisional assent from the reader because we like and wish to empathise with Austen's attractive main character and share her enjoyment of the follies of others, and therefore we are carried along and tricked into thinking she is offering objective judgement on Wickham and Darcy, especially as Elizabeth is right about all the other characters. There are examples on page 72: 'What could be the meaning of it? — It was impossible to imagine; it was impossible not to long to know' and on page 86: '...and to have Mr Collins instead!' This amalgam of narrator and heroine makes the reader identify closely with the latter and uncritically accept the feelings and views that she delivers with the authority of objective narrative. Coloured narrative is also used to convey collective thoughts of the community, as on page 12: 'What a contrast between him and his friend!' and on page 13: 'the proudest most disagreeable man in the world,' which also links with the **free indirect**

speech mode as the comments capture the likely expression of the gossip going around.

4 Character voice: dialogue

This mode constitutes the majority of the book, with coloured narrative coming second; the content of the novel is in fact around 90% dialogue. The purpose and effect of this narrative mode is to allow characters to reveal themselves entertainingly through the content and style of their speech, and it has the advantage of economy in that two or more characters can do so simultaneously. Characters amusingly and unwittingly condemn themselves out of their own mouths, and the reader can judge them without any need for help from the narrative voice. What they say is much more revealing of their beliefs and morals than any physical description can be. Those who are unwilling or unable to engage in genuine conversation, such as Mr Bennet, Mary, Lady Catherine and the early Darcy, can also be judged accordingly. Since the majority of dialogue necessarily takes the form of question and answer, characters can elicit information from each other on behalf of the reader.

As pairs or groups Austen's characters perform as if on stage, and in ever-changing combinations. This semi-formal mode of semi-public conversation has rules of engagement, so that characters can be judged by how well they adhere to them; Mr Collins and Lady Catherine fail by being too verbose and domineering respectively, and too self-regarding jointly. There is not only a variety of finely distinguished voices to be heard, but the dramatic effect of immediacy is created. Furthermore, dialogue provides scope for irony to function, as characters can convey the opposite impression to that which they intend, as well as reveal that they know less than the reader.

Dialogue advances the action and fleshes out the characters, and nothing is redundant. Plot elements, particularly intended movements, can be conveyed in this way, and set pieces of disagreement of viewpoints can be aired, such as that between Charlotte and Elizabeth on the subject of marriage, and between Darcy and Elizabeth on women's education. Hough argues that characters only ever reinforce the position the narrator has previously outlined for them and do not introduce anything new. This is not true in the case of Wickham however, as it is necessary for us, like Elizabeth, to initially draw our own conclusions based on hearing him speak. It has also been noted that dialogue is not used for intimate moments, as the author is more comfortable using this as a social rather than a private mode. Once couples have reached an understanding, exchanges between them serve no further purpose, and scenes of passion can be avoided by not allowing us to witness further intercourse.

5 Character voice: talking to oneself

To dramatise heightened moments characters are sometimes allowed to talk to themselves in direct speech. There is an example on page 182 where Elizabeth is

reliving the previous conversation with Colonel Fitzwilliam and her speech functions as the answer to him that she did not give at the time, and as an attempt to convince herself (by which she makes herself ill). Her reaction to Darcy's letter in Chapter 36 takes the same form of her 'repeatedly exclaiming, "This must be false!"' (p. 198), and on pages 201–02 she talks to herself for a whole paragraph to show the extent of her mental disturbance and feeling of humiliation. She talks, apparently aloud, to herself again in the opening of Chapter 54, until Jane arrives. Thoughts are also indicated by speech marks, as on page 212 when Elizabeth reacts to Lydia's plan to go to Brighton, and presumably her speech on page 322 is made only internally, since she is in public. In each case the turmoil of Elizabeth's mind or dislike of something is conveyed by this method.

6 Character voice: written speech

Letters are another mode of direct speech by a character, and can be seen as the written form of a character's voice as monologue — they are allowed to speak for much longer than would be considered realistic or polite as a contribution to a dialogue, and the lack of interruption enables the reader to focus on the one character and their viewpoint. This mode also allows plot information to be conveyed realistically, since letters are by definition used by one party to inform another about their whereabouts and the incidents in their current lives, and to describe events to someone who is not physically present. The reader can appreciate the situation of the writer but is positioned alongside the letter's recipient, so that we can also imagine and empathise with how they are feeling while they are reading it, and before we are actually told by the narrator how to respond. This is especially true when Elizabeth is reading her long letter from Darcy. The extensiveness of their utterance in a letter allows us to be able to form a clear judgement, based on a sufficient sample, of the characters' abilities as users of the English language, and to compare them with each other.

7 Character voice: incorporated speech

Austen sometimes quotes in speech marks part of the direct speech made by a character in an earlier conversation, allowing the reader to hear things that they were not privy to earlier. This device has the effect of doubling the time frame without losing the immediacy of it being the first time of utterance, as the earlier effect on the interlocutor can be imagined. Taken out of context these remarks can be made to seem silly or trivial, or to take on a gravity equal to a quotation from an authority figure, depending on character and context. There is an example on page 182 where Colonel Fitzwilliam is echoed in Elizabeth's review of the earlier conversation.

8 Character voice: speech within speech

Not widely used, one example occurs on page 103 when Mr Collins is telling Elizabeth his reasons for marrying and in doing so quotes the instruction of Lady

Catherine to find 'an active, useful sort of person' to marry. It enables both characters to be mocked simultaneously, her for saying such things and him for agreeing with them; the doubling of silly voices adds to the comic effect, and allows us to see similarities between the quoter and the quoted, as when Mrs Bennet tells us what her sister, Mrs Philips, said.

9 Character voice: free indirect speech

This is a hybrid style of third person narration combining the characteristics of reported speech with those of direct speech. Passages written using free indirect speech are often ambiguous as to whether they convey the views of the narrator or of the character the narrator is describing, creating an ironic interaction between internal and external perspectives. This device, which later came to be known as *style indirect libre*, is particularly associated with Austen's narrative technique, whereby the **ipsissima verba** of a character are incorporated into the narrative without inverted commas. The character's speech habits can be mocked in this way, as their expression is so readily identifiable within the more elegant and competent surrounding narrative style. This mode is used intermittently and in short passages throughout the novel.

Language and style

English language and usage has changed in various ways since the late eighteenth century. Some of these changes are easy to spot and not particularly significant, particularly those to do with **syntax** and punctuation (especially the abundance of commas) and spelling (Austen consistently spelt 'chuse', 'stile' and 'develope' thus, and words we now spell with 'ie' appear as 'ei', e.g. 'neice' and 'freindship'). The capitalisation of abstract nouns seems a trivial difference but was important in that such words as 'Evil', 'Honour', 'Principle' and 'Vice' stand out as having biblical connotations, and they therefore carry moral approbation or condemnation. Changes in the meanings of words are harder to identify and for that reason can mislead the reader into missing signs or wrongly interpreting them. Some of these are dealt with below.

It was a convention of the period to use fictitious place names for all but the major towns, and to leave blanks for some other proper names, e.g. on page 72. On page 211 there are blanks for both a town in Hertfordshire and the name of Wickham's regiment. London, Bath and Brighton are large enough be mentioned without fear of giving offence to any particular group of people. It was also common for dates to be left incomplete in contemporary novels; blanks fostered the illusion that the privacy of real people was being protected.

Austen's style is non-**figurative**, with few similes and metaphors, they being somewhat self-indulgent and suspect in the lucid and sensible world she creates.

There is little use of language that could be called **lyrical** or poetic, whereas there are many examples of typically eighteenth-century prose and essay devices, such as aphorism and **antithesis**, which she gives to her favoured characters: e.g. 'One has got all the goodness, and the other all the appearance of it.' (Elizabeth, p. 217) and 'his perfect indifference, and your pointed dislike, make it so delightfully absurd!' (Mr Bennet p. 344). In a letter to Cassandra, Austen referred to 'the playfulness & Epigrammatism of the general stile' of *Pride and Prejudice*.

Changed meanings

The evaluative vocabulary of approbation and condemnation of character behaviour is mostly in the form of certain adjectives that are used frequently in the novel. Readers can pick up the habit of moral discrimination by noting them and to whom they are applied. For example, 'proper', 'just' and 'serious' do not seem particularly 'loaded' now, but for Austen they were indicators of acceptable social behaviour and moral worth. Likewise, words such as 'giddy' or 'silly' may seem harmless or even attractively childlike to a modern reader, but it is strong criticism of Lydia and Kitty that their behaviour should be described in this way, meaning that they are deficient in consideration and moderation. The following words have also changed their meaning, are no longer in current use, or carried more moral weight than nowadays:

Elegant

This word is usually used critically to mean vain, and is applied particularly to women, particularly Londoners, who think too much of fashion and who try too hard to impress, such as Caroline Bingley. Mr Collins accuses Elizabeth of being an 'elegant female', which he implicitly defines as possessing 'affectation and coquetry' (p. 107). The word also appears in the novel in reference to someone's principles and manners rather than to their appearance. True elegance is of the mind and a goal to be aspired to, allied to the concepts of decorum, propriety and the other eighteenth-century virtues concerning thought, speech and behaviour; it is the opposite of vulgarity.

Sensibility

This can be defined as sentimental and emotional indulgence. The modern equivalent would be sensitivity, generally regarded now as a desirable trait, at least in controllable amounts. As an opposite of 'sense', however, it is seen as suspect in the works of Austen and in her characters. The desire to prove their sensibility, i.e. delicacy of feeling (as well as their over-tight corsetry) is what led women to faint at the drop of a hat and thus demonstrate their ladylike fragility during the decades that followed. Common sense and sound judgement are presented as being more worthy attributes than over-refined emotions, as sentimentality and emotional self-indulgence were considered dangerous and likely to lead to excess, error and other moral dangers. It is Elizabeth's sensibility that is piqued by Darcy's overheard comments and that leads her to make false judgements of him and Wickham. However, a complete lack of sensibility represents a woeful inability to feel appropriately and to be responsive to others; this is one of Mr Collins's deficiencies.

Vulgar

Meaning literally 'of the crowd', this was a term of disapprobation in a class-based society. It did not have the modern overtone of gross or rude, but was still a damaging assessment to make of someone, the equivalent of calling them 'common' and therefore lacking in taste and refinement. It is Mrs Bennet, her siblings and her younger daughters who are considered vulgar connections by the Bingley sisters and Lady Catherine (and they are right, except for her brother, Mr Gardiner), hence Caroline Bingley's jibe to Darcy that if he married Elizabeth he would be taking on 'vulgar relations'. One of Mrs Bennet's vulgar habits is to mention her servant Hill by name, as well as to refer often to food (mince pies and fish), and both she and her sister Mrs Philips are inveterate gossips. Mrs Philips is strongly condemned for her 'vulgarity' even at the end of the novel: 'whenever she did speak, she must be vulgar' (p. 363).

Gentleman

A word that came from the medieval idea of good breeding, it was used in Austen's time to denote someone belonging to the class of 'gentleman', one that was very important to her and to her characters. Darcy is horrified by Elizabeth's accusation that his conduct is unbecoming of a gentleman, and she also makes a point of telling Lady Catherine that she is a 'gentleman's daughter'. Originally meaning refined and courteous, 'gentil' evolved into the English word 'gentle', and the French and Italian for 'kind'. Gentle manners and behaviour were thought to be the product of noble birth and what distinguished the higher from the lower classes; however, Austen makes it clear that these qualities are a matter of upbringing and not of blood. A gentleman always paid his debts, so that Wickham's dereliction in this matter is a serious misdemeanour and makes him ungentlemanly, regardless of his social and professional status.

Duty

Duty (usually capitalised in Austen) conferred an obligation on a par with a religious imperative. Lady Catherine appeals to duty as a reason why Elizabeth cannot be allowed to marry her nephew. Duty to family was paramount and unquestioned, as was duty to hosts and guests, and an extension of the concept of duty was that of gratitude, which Mr Collins expects to be shown by the Bennets for his condescension in trying to marry one of the daughters to offset

the entail. Darcy continues to do his duty by Wickham, long after he would wish to have anything more to do with him, because the bond between their fathers obliges him to. A landowner also had a duty of care towards his estate workers, which included providing them with shelter. The social hierarchy of the period, descended from the feudal system, was only operable because everyone knew their place and did their duty, upwards and downwards. Elizabeth is also conscious of a duty to herself, which is why, unlike Charlotte, she will not agree to become the wife of Mr Collins, though this means overriding her duty to her parents. Fortunately her father relieves her of this obligation by saying he would disown her if she wanted to marry Mr Collins.

Stylistic traits

Adverbial intensifiers (e.g. 'extremely', 'exceedingly')

As a verbal redundancy, these adverbs of degree reveal a self-indulgence and lack of control of thought, emotion and deed; they are symptomatic of a lack of moderation and restraint to a writer who deplored excess and practised and preached Aristotle's golden mean. In her world view, extreme and inconcise expression is indicative of immoderate and rebellious tendencies that can lead to political revolution and chaos, the end of the old order, tradition and conservatism. It is fitting that Lydia, a breaker of rules, is at fault in this respect — as is her mother, who is unfamiliar with the very idea of moderation. Mrs Bennet favours the intensifier 'so' in front of adjectives, even when she is not comparing, as in 'so pleased', 'so happy', 'so handsome', 'so tall'. Superlatives and hyperbole indicate a jumping to conclusions and error of judgement, as in 'He was the proudest, most disagreeable man in the world'.

Question marks, exclamations and dashes

Punctuation is as revealing as vocabulary in the speech patterns of Austen's characters. Vivacity is suspect, since it argues a lack of seriousness, meaning that characters whose speech is dotted with attention-seeking question and exclamation marks are being overdramatic and showing off, as well as revealing a lack of previous reflection on their utterances. Mrs Bennet's speech at the bottom of page 43, which includes dashes as well as exclamations and questions, shows a sloppiness and want of syntactical organisation that, by definition, gives the impression of casual rather than sophisticated speech. Lydia's rambling monologue on pages 213–14 is not only full of grammatical errors, exaggerations and vulgar expressions (such as 'Lord!' and 'you can't think') but also consists entirely of names and exclamations (and simple or compound sentences). Kitty also uses the exclamatory monosyllable 'La!' as an affectation. The fact that Darcy's letter in Chapter 35 contains so many dashes (and so many sentences beginning with 'But') can only be explained by his being in a highly perturbed state and unable, for once, to collect and organise his thoughts before uttering them. The effect is to show the reader and Elizabeth a very different Darcy and to signal that he will be less reserved in the second half of the novel. The dashes become fewer as the letter progresses, however, as if he has become calmer with the writing of it.

Triple syntactical structures

'She was a woman of mean understanding, little information, and uncertain temper' (Chapter 1). This description of Mrs Bennet as a list of three adjective/noun phrases was considered the elegant way to construct sentences — and modelled by the arbiter of good style, Dr Johnson — and was applied to single words, phrases or clauses. The author and her intelligent, educated or socially superior characters speak in triples: Elizabeth laments that Darcy should stoop to 'such malicious revenge, such injustice, such inhumanity' towards 'the godson, the friend, the favourite of his father' (p. 79), describes Bingley as 'sweet tempered, amiable, charming' (p. 81), and attacks Darcy for telling her that he likes her 'against your will, against your reason, and even against your character' (p. 186). Mrs Gardiner says 'so hackneyed, so doubtful, so indefinite' (p. 138) and 'a violation of decency, honour, and interest'; Mr Gardiner describes Darcy as 'perfectly well behaved, polite and unassuming' (p. 246); even Lady Catherine threatens that Elizabeth 'will be censured, slighted, and despised' (p. 336) for being 'a young woman without family, connections, or fortune' (p. 337) who refuses 'to obey the claims of duty, honour, and gratitude' (p. 338). It is because Wickham can adopt this measured, sophisticated and argumentatively powerful style that he deceives Elizabeth and the reader. The use of three is still advised for persuasive rhetoric and is much beloved of politicians: four would be too many, too list-like; two would be insufficient and unconvincing — three is the perfect balance between excess and deficiency.

Concrete and domestic nouns

The content of a character's speech is as revealing as their style and even more obvious. Polite and educated discourse consisted of discussion of ideas rather than things, and especially not things of a quotidian, mundane and domestic nature, especially when dancing. Instead the abstract nouns of morality — such as sense, courage, fortitude, vanity, folly, reason — were unashamedly and continually discussed to raise the tone of conversation. Mr Collins peppers his pontificating pronouncements with self-aggrandising abstracts but ruins the effect they might otherwise have by descending into the prosaic details of the decor at Rosings (such as its £800 chimney-piece) and its inhabitants, cuisine and environs, which reveals his spiritual poverty as surely as certain members of the Bennet family reveal theirs through talk of bonnets, barouches, and the colour of Wickham's coat. Lydia is more concerned about her wedding clothes than her choice of husband or her reputation, and instructs Harriet Forster to instruct the servant Sally to mend the

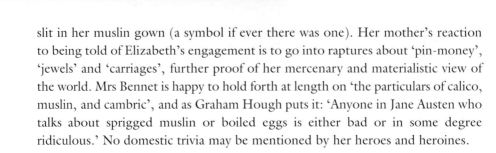

slit in her muslin gown (a symbol if ever there was one). Her mother's reaction to being told of Elizabeth's engagement is to go into raptures about 'pin-money', 'jewels' and 'carriages', further proof of her mercenary and materialistic view of the world. Mrs Bennet is happy to hold forth at length on 'the particulars of calico, muslin, and cambric', and as Graham Hough puts it: 'Anyone in Jane Austen who talks about sprigged muslin or boiled eggs is either bad or in some degree ridiculous.' No domestic trivia may be mentioned by her heroes and heroines.

Non-sentences, simple or compound sentences

As one would expect, Mrs Bennet is the main offender. On page 14 she cannot form a complex sentence, as shown by the frequency of semi-colons and her reliance on 'and' as a simple coordinator. Her speech on the next page includes 'excessively', a common cant intensifier (and references to 'dresses', 'lace' and 'gown', which are so tedious that her husband interrupts her) and exclamations, non-sentences and hyperbolic language: 'never in my life', 'horrid' and 'detest'. On page 357 she is barely able to form a sentence of any kind, as indicated by the dashes which precede the **anacoluthon** (incomplete syntax).

Idiolects

Most novelists distinguish between class and gender in terms of topic of conversation, but few go in for the subtle gradations and idiosyncrasies of style that Austen goes in for, even within the same social group. Though we cannot know the standards of normal speech before the invention of the tape recorder, we can know from **intratextual** comparison whether a character is to be considered affected, pompous, natural, vulgar, etc. The whole range of dialect and **accented** popular speech is excluded (unlike in Dickens, for instance) so the scale is narrow, but this allows for fine distinctions within moderately educated speech and polite conversation, so that every nuance and deviation is indicative of attitude and moral status. Austen chastised her niece Anna for giving a 'too familiar & inelegant' phrase ('Bless my heart') to a character in her writing whom she wished to be considered proper. Bingley accuses Darcy of using 'words of four syllables', which reflects the latter's intellectual habits, stiffness of mien and lack of ease in speech, the opposite of his friend's mode of conversing. Mr Collins uses clichés that reveal his shallowness, insensitivity to language and lack of creativity; he is a man who refuses to read novels. His use of **litotes**, e.g. 'will not fail of being acceptable' (p. 106) and 'not disagreeably' (p. 208), and over-long and convoluted sentences, with all their unnecessary passives and double negatives, are evidence of a prolixity that relates to pomposity. Just as some characters cause shame for others with their way of talking, the author attacks her characters by giving them unsuitable modes of expression.

Critical comments

Austen's own comments in letters

- I must confess that I think [Elizabeth Bennet] as delightful a creature as ever appeared in print. (*29 January 1813 to Cassandra*)

- I do not write for such dull elves / As have not a great deal of ingenuity themselves. (*ibid.*)

- [*Pride and Prejudice*] is rather too light, and bright, and sparkling; it wants shade; it wants to be stretched out here and there with a long chapter of sense. (*4 February 1813 to Cassandra*)

- 3 or 4 Families in a Country Village is the very thing to work on. (*9 September 1814 to Anna Austen*)

- Pictures of perfection as you know make me sick & wicked. (*23 March 1816 to Fanny Knight*)

- I think I may boast myself to be [...] the most unlearned and uninformed female who ever dared to be an authoress. (*11 December 1815 to James Stanier Clarke, chaplain and librarian to the Prince of Wales*)

- ...the little bit (two Inches wide) of Ivory on which I work with so fine a Brush, as produces little effect after much labour. (*16 December 1816 to nephew James Edward Austen*)

Nineteenth-century critics

- Among the writers who [...] have approached nearest to the manner of [Shakespeare's characterisation] we have no hesitation in placing Jane Austen.

  Thomas Macaulay, 1843

- Miss Austen [...] cannot be great. [...] The Passions are perfectly unknown to Jane Austen.

  Charlotte Brontë, 1850

- A carefully fenced, highly cultivated garden, with neat borders and delicate flowers; but no glance of a bright, vivid physiognomy, no open country, no fresh air, no blue hill, no bonny beck.

  (*idem*)

- Her circle may be restricted, but it is complete. Her world is a perfect orb, and vital.

  George Henry Lewes, 1852

- Perfect [characters] as far as they go — that's certain. Only they don't go far, I think.

  Elizabeth Barrett Browning, 1855

- Vulgar in tone, sterile in artistic invention, imprisoned in the wretched conventions of English society, without genius, wit, or knowledge of the world. Never was life so pinched and narrow.

  Ralph Waldo Emerson, 1861

- She is capital as far as she goes: but she never goes out of the Parlour.

  Edward Fitzgerald, 1875

Twentieth-century critics

- Little touches of human truth, little glimpses of steady vision, little master-strokes of imagination
  Henry James, 1905

- Jane is entirely impossible. It seems a great pity that they allowed her to die a natural death.
  (*idem*)

- Whenever I take up Pride and Prejudice [...] I feel like a barkeeper entering the Kingdom of Heaven.
  Mark Twain, 1909

- Jane Austen is [...] a mistress of much deeper emotion than appears on the surface. She stimulates us to supply what is not there.
  Virginia Woolf, 1925

- Whatever she writes is finished and turned and set in its relation, not to the parsonage, but to the universe. She is impersonal; she is inscrutable.
  (*idem*)

- Physical violence is quite beyond Miss Austen's powers [...] [she is] 'feeble and ladylike'.
  E. M. Forster, 1927

- All the Jane Austen characters are ready for an extended life, for a life which the scheme of her books seldom requires them to lead, and that is why they lead their actual lives so satisfactorily.
  (*idem*)

- An exquisite mastery of whatever can be mastered.
  André Gide, 1929

- ...thoroughly unpleasant, English in the bad, mean, snobbish sense of the word.
  D. H. Lawrence, 1930

- Miss Austen is almost unique among the novelists of her sex in being deeply and steadily concerned [...] as the great masculine novelists are, with the novel as a work of art.
  Edmund Wilson, 1945

- At the height of political and industrial revolution, in a decade of formidable philosophic activity, Miss Austen composes novels almost extra-terrestrial to history.
  George Steiner, 1975

Useful quotations

The best quotations to know are those that you have found useful in class discussions and practice essays, and they will require little conscious learning because you are already familiar with them. The most effective ones to learn in addition are those that serve more than one purpose, i.e. that can be used to support a theme or style usage as well as a point about character.

It is a truth universally acknowledged, that a single man in possession of a good fortune, must be in want of a wife. (*First sentence, p. 5*)

'...she is not half so handsome as Jane, nor half so good humoured as Lydia.' (*Mrs Bennet to Mr Bennet about Elizabeth, p. 6*)

'Lizzy has something more of quickness than her sisters. (*Mr Bennet to Mrs Bennet, p. 7*)

She was a woman of mean understanding, little information, and uncertain temper. (*About Mrs Bennet, p. 7*)

'You are dancing with the only handsome girl in the room.' (*Darcy to Bingley about Jane, p. 13*)

'She is tolerable; but not handsome enough to tempt me.' (*Darcy to Bingley about Elizabeth, p. 13*)

...for she had a lively, playful disposition, which delighted in anything ridiculous. (*About Elizabeth, p. 14*)

'you are a great deal too apt, you know, to like people in general. You never see a fault in anybody.' (*Elizabeth to Jane, p. 16*)

'I could easily forgive his pride, if he had not mortified mine.' (*Elizabeth to Charlotte about Darcy, p. 21*)

'Pride [...] is a very common failing, I believe.' (*Mary to herself, p. 21*)

'Happiness in marriage is entirely a matter of chance [...] and it is better to know as little as possible of the defects of the person with whom you are to pass your life.' (*Charlotte to Elizabeth, p. 24*)

'I have been meditating on the very great pleasure which a pair of fine eyes in the face of a pretty woman can bestow.' (*Darcy to Miss Bingley about Elizabeth, p. 27*)

'Whatever bears affinity to cunning is despicable.' (*Darcy to Miss Bingley, p. 40*)

Darcy had never been so bewitched by any woman as he was by her. He really believed, that were it not for the inferiority of her connections, he should be in some danger. (*About Elizabeth, p. 51*)

'I dearly love a laugh.' (*Elizabeth, p. 56*)

'There is, I believe, in every disposition a tendency to some particular evil, a natural defect, which not even the best education can overcome.' (*Darcy to Elizabeth, p. 57*)

'Can he be a sensible man, sir?' (*Elizabeth to her father about Mr Collins, p. 63*)

'There is a mixture of servility and self-importance in his letter, which promises well.' (*Mr Bennet to Elizabeth about Mr Collins, p. 63*)

Mr. Collins had only to change from Jane to Elizabeth — and it was soon done — done while Mrs. Bennet was stirring the fire. (*p. 70*)

'It is particularly incumbent on those who never change their opinion, to be secure of judging properly at first.' (*Elizabeth to Darcy, p. 92*)

'Do not consider me now as an elegant female, intending to plague you, but as a rational creature, speaking the truth from her heart.' (*Elizabeth to Mr Collins, p. 106*)

'Your mother will never see you again if you do not marry Mr. Collins, and I will never see you again if you do.' (*Mr Bennet to Elizabeth, p. 110*)

'The more I see of the world, the more am I dissatisfied with it; and every day confirms my belief of the inconsistency of all human characters, and of the little dependence that can be placed on the appearance of merit or sense.' (*Elizabeth to Jane, p. 133*)

'Mr. Collins is a conceited, pompous, narrow-minded, silly man; you know he is, as well as I do; and you must feel, as well as I do, that the woman who marries him cannot have a proper way of thinking.' (*Elizabeth to Charlotte, p. 133*)

'Let our first effusions be less insupportable than those of the generality of travellers.' (*Elizabeth to Mrs Gardiner, p. 152*)

'And is this all?' cried Elizabeth. 'I expected at least that the pigs were got into the garden, and here is nothing but Lady Catherine and her daughter.' (*p. 156*)

'There is a stubbornness about me that never can bear to be frightened at the will of others. My courage always rises with every attempt to intimidate me.' (*Elizabeth, p. 170*)

'In vain have I struggled. It will not do. My feelings will not be repressed. You must allow me to tell you how ardently I admire and love you.' (*Darcy to Elizabeth, p. 185*)

'Do you think that any consideration would tempt me to accept the man, who has been the means of ruining, perhaps for ever, the happiness of a most beloved sister?' (*Elizabeth to Darcy, p. 186*)

'Could you expect me to rejoice in the inferiority of your connections? — to congratulate myself on the hope of relations, whose condition in life is so decidedly beneath my own?' (*Darcy to Elizabeth, p. 188*)

'I had not known you a month before I felt that you were the last man in the world whom I could ever be prevailed on to marry.' (*Elizabeth to Darcy, p. 188*)

He expressed no regret for what he had done which satisfied her; his style was not penitent, but haughty. It was all pride and insolence. (*Elizabeth about Darcy's letter, p. 198*)

Of neither Darcy or Wickham could she think, without feeling that she had been blind, partial, prejudiced, absurd. (*Elizabeth, p. 201*)

'Till this moment, I never knew myself.' (*Elizabeth to herself, p. 202*)

'...it is many months since I have considered her as one of the handsomest women of my acquaintance.' (*Darcy to Miss Bingley about Elizabeth, p. 259*)

'Wretched, wretched mistake!' (*Elizabeth to Darcy about not having passed on what she knew about Wickham, p. 264*)

'The death of your daughter would have been a blessing in comparison of this.' (*Mr Collins in a letter to Mr Bennet, p. 281*)

'...obstinacy is the real defect of his character after all. He has been accused of many faults at different times; but this is the true one.' (*Mrs Gardiner in a letter to Elizabeth about Darcy, p. 306*)

'...the upstart pretensions of a young woman without family, connections, or fortunes.' (*Lady Catherine attacking Elizabeth, p. 337*)

'He is a gentleman; I am a gentleman's daughter; so far we are equal.' (*Elizabeth to Lady Catherine about Darcy, p. 337*)

'For what do we live, but to make sport for our neighbours, and laugh at them in our turn?' (*Mr Bennet to Elizabeth, p. 343–44*)

...he expressed himself on the occasion as sensibly and as warmly as a man violently in love can be supposed to do. (*About Darcy, p. 346*)

'The conduct of neither, if strictly examined, will be irreproachable; but since then, we have both, I hope, improved in civility.' (*Elizabeth to Darcy, p. 347*)

'As a child I was taught what was right, but I was not taught to correct my temper. I was given good principles, but left to follow them in pride and conceit.' (*Darcy to Elizabeth, p. 349*)

'What do I not owe you! You taught me a lesson, hard indeed at first, but most advantageous. By you, I was properly humbled.' (*Darcy to Elizabeth, p. 349*)

'I believe I must date it from my first seeing his beautiful grounds at Pemberley.' (*Elizabeth to Jane about falling in love with Darcy, p. 353*)

Literary terms and concepts

The terms and concepts below have been selected for their relevance to talking and writing about *Pride and Prejudice*. It is a requirement of AO1 to use 'appropriate terminology and concepts', and it will aid argument and expression to become familiar with them and to use them in discussion and essays.

accent	features of pronunciation that vary according to the speaker's regional and social origin
anacoluthon	syntactical breakdown whereby what follows is ungrammatical
anagnorisis	moment of recognition by a character of an important truth
antithesis	contrasting of ideas by balancing words or phrases of opposite meaning, e.g. 'her jealousy and dislike of one sister much exceeded her affection for the other'
aphorism	tersely phrased statement of a truth or opinion
authorial voice	interpolation by the author that is distinct from the narrator's voice
bathos	sudden change of register from the important to the ridiculously trivial, with comic effect, e.g. Mrs Bennet changing the conversation mid-flow from daughters losing potential husbands to 'long sleeves'
bourgeois	typical of, and conforming to, middle-class attitudes and conventions of respectability and materialism; in Marxist theory, a member of the property-owning class
broadsheet	posters and handbills on topical subjects, circulated especially in the eighteenth century, often satirical
caricature	exaggerated and mocking portrayal of a person built around a specific physical, verbal or character trait
characterisation	means by which fictional characters are personified and made distinctive
classical	Ancient Greek or Roman artistic style and content, typified by a restraint of feelings and regularity of form; particularly popular in the eighteenth century
cliché	predictable and overused expression or situation

climax	moment of intensity to which a series of events has been leading
closure	sense of an ending and completeness; tying up the loose ends in a fictional work
comedy	fictional work in which confusions and deceptions are unravelled, with amusement along the way, ending in resolution, restitution and reconciliation
comedy of errors	a ludicrous situation in which mistakes are made and things go wrong
comedy of humours	closely associated with the early seventeenth-century playwright Ben Jonson, a comedy focusing on characters with a dominant trait caused by an excess of one of the four humours
comedy of manners	comedy satirising the attitudes and behaviour of a particular social group, usually one that considers itself fashionable
contextuality	historical, social and cultural background of a text
denouement	unfolding of the final stages of a plot, when all is revealed
dialogue	direct speech of characters engaged in conversation
diction	choice of vocabulary from a particular category
didactic	with the intention of teaching the reader and instilling moral values
drama	composition in verse or prose, involving conflict, which is performed through action and dialogue
dramatic irony	when the audience knows something that the character speaking does not, which creates humour or tension
Electra complex	psychoanalytical term to describe a girl's romantic feelings toward her father; from a character in Greek tragedy; opposite of Oedipus complex
empathy	identifying with a character in a literary work
Enlightenment	philosophical movement of the eighteenth century that emphasised rationality, scientific thought and human rights; it led to the rise of democracy and contributed to the French and American Revolutions
epigram	a short, concise, original and witty expression
epistolary	story told entirely in the form of letters exchanged between participating or observing characters; common eighteenth-century novel genre

eponymous	main character after whom a work is named, e.g. *Sir Charles Grandison*
euphemism	tactful word or phrase used to refer to something embarrassing or offensive, e.g. 'woman of the town' for prostitute
evangelical	relating to a religious group that stresses personal conversion and salvation by faith; characterised by zealous enthusiasm and ardent crusading
femme fatale	sensuous and alluring woman who seduces men
figurative	using imagery; non-literal use of language
flat and round	terms coined by E. M. Forster to distinguish between fictional characters capable of surprising the reader (round) and those entirely consistent and predictable (flat)
flawed lens	a narrative viewpoint that is untrustworthy because the narrator is partially blinded by prejudice or ignorance
free indirect speech	also known as *le style indirect libre* or *erlebte Rede*, the use in narrative of a character's spoken words, without attribution or inverted commas; blend of first and third person discourse
genre	type or form of writing with identifiable characteristics, e.g. fairy tale
golden mean	Aristotle's philosophy of moderation and balance in temperament; desirable middle between the two extremes of deficiency and excess
Gothic	cruel passions and supernatural terrors in a medieval setting or gloomy atmosphere; popular genre at the end of the eighteenth and throughout the nineteenth centuries
humours	relating to medieval belief that four human character types — melancholic, choleric, sanguine or phlegmatic — were caused by an excess of one of the four bodily fluids: black bile; yellow bile, blood and phlegm respectively
hyperbole	deliberate exaggeration for effect
idiolect	style of speech peculiar to an individual character and recognisable as such
imagery	descriptive language appealing to the senses, usually in the form of simile or metaphor; may be sustained or recurring throughout texts
interlocutor	partner in dialogue

intertextuality	relationship between one text and another
intratextuality	system of self-reference within a text, which does not relate to reality but only to its own constructed patterns; language use by characters is evaluated intra-textually in Austen's works
ipsissima verba	literally 'the very same words', a Latin phrase used to refer to the free indirect speech mode whereby the character's voice can be heard within the narrative
irony	language intended to mean the opposite of the words expressed; or amusing or cruel reversal of an outcome expected, intended or deserved; situation in which one is mocked by fate or the facts
Jacobin	sympathiser with radical principles; follower of the revolutionary group founded in 1789 in Paris under the leadership of Robespierre
juvenilia	works produced by an author or artist in youth
lèse majesté	an affront to the dignity of a ruler of importance
litotes	expressing an affirmative by the negative of its contrary, e.g. 'not inconsiderable'; Mr Collins uses this prolix and affected stylistic trait
lyrical	expression of strong feelings, usually love; suggestive of music
monologue	extended speech or thought process by one character; a letter reproduced in full is a form of monologue
motif	recurring structural or literary device that develops and informs a text's major themes e.g. references to income per annum
narrative	connected, and usually chronological, series of events that form a story
noblesse oblige	benevolent, honourable behaviour considered to be the duty of persons of high birth and rank
omniscient narrator	storyteller with total knowledge of events and characters' thoughts
oxymoron	two contradictory terms united in a single phrase, often for comic effect e.g. 'dignified impertinence'
parody	imitation and exaggeration of style for purpose of humour and ridicule
peripeteia	sudden reversal of fortune in either tragedy or comedy; an abrupt rise or fall and change of circumstances for a main character

picaresque	a genre of usually satiric prose fiction depicting in realistic and often humorous detail the adventures of a roguish hero of low class living by his/her wits in a corrupt society
Platonic love	Ancient Greek philosopher's view that perfect love involves finding one's other half; the elevation of the soul and the achievement of excellence through a pure, noble, spiritual relationship that enables both lover and beloved to improve in the search for virtue
plot	cause-and-effect sequence of events caused by characters' actions
poetic justice	appropriate and often ironic rewarding of virtue and punishing of vice in fiction
posthumous	published after the writer's death
realism	associated with the rise of the novel in the early eighteenth century, realism refers to the depiction of detailed, accurately observed scenery, objects, characters and behaviours; it contrasts with **idealism**, which filters out unpalatable realities and individual experience or perception
register	level of formality; form of speech shaped by social context
rhetoric	art of persuasion using emotive language and stylistic devices, e.g. triple structures
romance	story of love and heroism, deriving from medieval court life and fairy tale
Romanticism	influential artistic movement of the late eighteenth and early nineteenth centuries, characterised by the rebellious assertion of the individual and a belief in the spiritual correspondence between man and nature
satire	exposing of the vice or foolishness of a person or institution to ridicule
seven Christian virtues	faith, hope, charity, justice, fortitude, prudence and temperance; these are at the forefront of Austen's didactic mission
seven deadly sins	the medieval Catholic church preached that these sins were mortal and led straight to hell: pride, envy, gluttony, lechery, avarice, wrath, sloth
stereotype	a category of person with recognisably typical characteristics, often the target of mockery

style	selection and organisation of language elements, determined by genre or individual user of language
symbol	object, person or event that represents an abstract idea greater than itself
syntax	choice of grammar and word order in sentence construction
theme	abstract and universal idea or issue explored in a text, which is fundamental to its purpose or meaning
tone	emotional aspect of the voice of a text, e.g. 'sarcastic', 'exuberant'
wit	intelligent verbal humour

Questions & Answers

Essay questions

The secret of exam essay success is a good plan, which gives coverage and exploration of the title and refers to the four elements of text: plot, characterisation, language, and themes. Think about the issues freshly rather than attempting to regurgitate your own or someone else's ideas, and avoid giving the impression of a pre-packaged or all-purpose essay you are determined to deliver whatever the title.

When you've chosen a question, underline its key words and define them briefly, in as many ways as are relevant to the text, to form the introduction and provide the background. Plan the rest of the essay, staying focused on the question, in approximately 12 points, recorded as short phrases with indication of support. Include a concluding point that does not repeat anything already said but that pulls your ideas together to form an overview. It may refer to other readers' opinions, refer back to the title, or include a relevant quotation from the text or elsewhere.

Check your plan to make sure you have dealt with all parts of the question, have used examples of the four elements of text in your support, and have analysed, not just described. Remind yourself of the Assessment Objectives (printed on the exam paper). Group points and organise the plan into a structure with numbers, brackets or arrows.

Tick off the points in your plan as you use them in the writing of your essay, and put a diagonal line through the whole plan once you have finished. You can add extra material as you write, as long as it does not take you away from the outline you have constructed or cause you to contradict your argument. Concentrate on expressing yourself clearly as you write your essay, and on writing concisely and precisely (e.g. 'Mr Bennet has the wrong priorities in putting amusement and a quiet life before his paternal responsibilities' is more specific and will be more highly rewarded than 'Mr Bennet is not a good father'). Integrate short quotations throughout the essay.

Allow five minutes at the end for checking and improving your essay in content and style. Insertions and crossings-out, if legible, are to be encouraged. As well as checking accuracy of spelling, grammar and punctuation, watch out for errors of fact, name or genre slips, repetition, and absence of linkage between paragraphs. Make sure your conclusion sounds conclusive, and not as though you've run out of time, ideas or ink. A few minutes spent checking can make the difference of a grade.

Planning practice

Using some of the titles from the section below, practise planning essay titles within a time limit of eight minutes, using about half a page. Aim for at least ten points and know how you would support them. Use numbers to structure the plan. Do this in groups and exchange and compare plans. Get used to using note form and abbreviations for names to save time. Since beginnings are the most daunting part of the essay for many students, you should also practise opening paragraphs for your planned essays. Remember to define the terms of the title, especially any abstract words, and this will give your essay breadth, depth and structure, e.g. if the word 'education' appears, say exactly what you take 'education' to mean, and how many different things it can mean in the context of the novel. Students also often find conclusions difficult, so experiment with final paragraphs for the essays you have planned. The whole essay is working towards the conclusion, so you need to know what it is going to be before you start writing the essay, and to make it clear that you have proved your case, whatever it may be.

Examiners advise that reference to the rest of the work should be as much as 60% of the essay even for a passage-based question. Focus closely on the passage, but also relate its content and/or language to elsewhere in the text and link your comments to the overall themes and/or structure of the novel. Include references to character, event, theme and language, and ask how the episode modifies or adds to our understanding so far, and how typical it is of the work as a whole. Think about reader reaction, using your own as the basis for your response. Here are the questions to address when analysing a passage from a novel:

- Why has the author included this passage? What is its importance?
- How does this passage fit into the narrative structure?
- Is it primarily looking forward to something that is to come, or looking backwards to explain or reinforce a previous event?
- Which of the novel's themes are being evoked, and how does this passage fit into the treatment of those themes as a whole?
- What previous scenes or events do we need to recall in order to fully understand the implications of this passage?
- How does this passage relate to elsewhere? Is it similar or a contrast to another episode?
- Does this extract foreshadow any future scenes or events?
- Which narrative modes are being employed at this point?
- How might modern readers react differently from early nineteenth-century readers to the content of this passage?
- What does this passage reveal about the characters and their feelings and thoughts?
- Is any information that the reader is aware or not aware of being withheld at this point?
- Are there any recurring images, symbols or motifs in this passage? If so, how do they fit into the overall pattern.
- If there is description, what mood is being evoked, and how?
- If there is dialogue, what does its content, style and tone tell us about the speakers?
- If there are entrances and/or exits, what effect do they have on the atmosphere?

- Where is the audience's sympathy, and why?
- How does narrative viewpoint affect the audience's feelings about something or someone?
- Whose is the voice in this passage, and what is the effect?
- What can be said about style, including generic conventions, choice of diction, sentence structure and punctuation?

A Passage-based questions: prescribed

1 How does Austen tell the story in Chapter 19?

2 Reread Chapter 46. 'The passions are perfectly unknown to Jane Austen.' Do you think that Charlotte Brontë's judgement on the author of *Pride and Prejudice* is a fair one, based on the evidence of this passage?

3 Remind yourself of the letter in Chapter 52, from Mrs Gardiner to Elizabeth. With reference to this letter, comment on the role played by letters in *Pride and Prejudice*.

4 How well does the presentation of Darcy in Chapter 8 prepare the reader for his later role and actions in the novel?

5 Reread Chapter 5. Explore Austen's presentation of family and country life.

6 Remind yourself of Chapter 21. How does this chapter highlight the differences in character between Elizabeth and Jane?

7 Remind yourself of Chapter 16, from the arrival of Wickham. How does Austen present Elizabeth and Wickham and the relationship between them here?

8 Look again at Chapter 49. Based on this chapter, including Mr Gardiner's letter, comment on the part money and property play in the novel as a whole.

9 Reread Chapter 41, to the bottom of p. 224, about Lydia's departure for Brighton. What is the role of the regiment and of Brighton in the novel?

10 Reread the passage in which Elizabeth and Charlotte discuss the latter's acceptance of Mr Collins's proposal in Chapter 22. What do you find interesting about the ways in which this marriage is presented, and what does it contribute to the novel's attitude to marriage in general?

11 Reread Chapter 39. Comment on Lydia's character and her relationship with her sisters.

B Whole-novel questions

1 What importance does Mr Collins have in the whole of *Pride and Prejudice*?

2 Examine the novel's presentation of the distinctions and relations between different social groups.

3 'In *Pride and Prejudice*, marriage is presented primarily as an economic arrangement.' How far and in what ways do you agree with this view?

4 'Irony is central to the meaning and effects of *Pride and Prejudice*.' How far and in what ways do you find this to be the case?

5 'Austen examines serious topics but always in a comic mode'. How do you respond to this statement? Discuss the novel's narrative method with reference to particular scenes.

6 'It is personal conduct rather than personal relationships which preoccupy Austen.' Examine the conduct and relationships of at least three appropriate characters in *Pride and Prejudice* in the light of this claim.

7 '*Pride and Prejudice* is basically just a Cinderella story of a girl who rises above her social destiny.' Discuss this dismissive view of the novel and its heroine, with particular reference to the narrative method.

8 Explore the novel's presentation of courtship and marriage with reference to three actual or potential marriages.

9 'She is one of the most consistent satirists in the whole of literature.' Discuss Virginia Woolf's view of Austen as a satirist with reference to *Pride and Prejudice*.

10 'A man changes his manners and a young lady changes her mind'. Say whether you think Tony Tanner's summary of *Pride and Prejudice* is adequate.

11 Vivien Jones says in the introduction to the novel 'Like its protagonists, *Pride and Prejudice* is vitally engaged in argument.' Describe some of the arguments of both the novel and its protagonists, and show how they relate to each other.

12 Do you believe Austen manages 'to reconcile vivacity of spirits with sobriety of judgement' in *Pride and Prejudice*? Explain how you think she succeeds or why she fails to.

13 In *Pride and Prejudice* 'money and rank place people on the social map as precisely as a grid reference'. To what extent do you agree with this statement?

14 With reference to two or three couples, show what *Pride and Prejudice* tells us of relations between men and women, and of what makes a perfect union between them.

15 D. W. Harding said that the novel shows 'concern with the survival of the sensitive and penetrating individual in a society of conforming mediocrity.' Comment on all the aspects and implications of this quotation.

16 'She is a miniaturist, but never two-dimensional. All her characters are round, or capable of rotundity.' Do you agree with E. M. Forster that all the characters in *Pride and Prejudice* avoid being caricatures? Discuss Austen's characterisation with reference to three minor characters.

C Comparative questions (with either *The French Lieutenant's Woman* or *The Yellow Wallpaper*)

1 'Female characters are often represented as being constrained by their societies.' Explore the presentation of female characters in the light of this statement.

In your response you should focus on *Pride and Prejudice* to establish your argument, and you should refer to the second text you have read to support and develop your line of argument.

2 'There is always a huge contrast between the behaviour of men and women.' Using *Pride and Prejudice*, Chapter 19, p. 104 as your starting point from '"You are too hasty, sir," she cried' to '"as would be consistent with the true delicacy of the female character"' at the bottom of p. 105, explore the presentation of the behaviour of men and women.

In your response you should focus on *Pride and Prejudice* to establish your argument, and you should refer to the second text you have read to support and develop your line of argument.

Sample questions with notes

A Passage-based questions: prescribed

1 How does Austen tell the story in Chapter 19?

Top band descriptors
AO2 exploration and analysis of key aspects of form, with perceptive evaluation of how they shape meanings.

Possible content
Reference might be made to the novel's form, a romance, a social comedy, a family saga, etc.; actual chapter reads like a comic set piece structure narrative frame with its focus on Elizabeth — Austen announces the proposal at the start of the chapter so there is no narrative surprise, dramatic climax — the proposal and Elizabeth's refusal, Austen's concluding paragraph acting as a commentary; omniscient third person narrator but with a focus on Elizabeth's consciousness; setting — the enclosed downstairs room; language — formal Latinate style, contrast of E's early panic with Collins's self assurance, use of the word 'insist' by Mrs Bennet, measured narrative of JA in contrast to the prolix style of Collins, use of verbs of saying, 'she cried' and adverbial phrase 'with some warmth', use of questions, exclamations, irony, etc.

2 Reread Chapter 46. 'The passions are perfectly unknown to Jane Austen.' Do you think that Charlotte Brontë's judgement on the author of *Pride and Prejudice* is a fair one, based on the evidence of this passage?

Possible plan
- Define passion: strong opinion, feeling, erotic or physical response
- Brontë's view is affected by considerations of natural environment/Romanticism/ use of first person; JA uses none of these.
- Head vs heart dichotomy; JA generally gives impression that head more important.
- Comedy concerned with thinking not feeling; humour and irony are deflaters of passion.
- No dialogue directly about passion in JA, unlike between Jane and Rochester in *Jane Eyre*.

- Passion suspect because an assertion of the individual against society; superficially passionate characters turn out to be shallow, selfish, destructive, and held up for our contempt rather than admiration, because their feelings untempered by judgement, e.g. Lydia and Wickham.

- Those who suffer in silence ask for our admiration, and appeal for our understanding that theirs are the truer, deeper passions, e.g. Darcy 'In vain have I struggled [...] My feelings will not be repressed'.

- Regulated passion is nonetheless feeling, and so strong it needs regulation; expression in measured syntax and tone does not mean feeling is negligible; enforced reticence required in the social context.

- However, seemingly trivial matters are transformed into important ethical dilemmas; JA and her heroines are passionate about morality.

- Passion does not have to include physical contact; other meaning of word is suffering, connected to 'patient' and 'passive', all relevant to Elizabeth's situation.

- P & P a love story, with usual passions of true love not running smooth: family and social obstacles; thwarting and anguish, suffering and waiting, 'repining'.

- Letters are usually distanced from feeling because written after reflection but in this chapter Jane's letter was written in the heat of the moment and is full of exclamations, dashes and is barely legible because of her emotional state, the more striking because we don't see Jane betraying emotion elsewhere — JA has saved it for dramatic effect.

- Many conflicting emotions in this chapter cause E. to forget herself and indulge in violent physical exertion, e.g. 'darting from her seat', similar to when she walked to Netherfield in defiance of convention to see her dangerously ill sister.

- E. often makes herself ill because of the strength of her emotions, and does so in this chapter when she bursts into tears, has to be supported to prevent her from fainting, puts a handkerchief over her face to hide her despair.

- Words used in this chapter (often more than once) are 'wild', 'compassionate', 'agitated', 'astonishment', 'grieved', 'shocked', 'distress', 'misery', 'horror': all strong passions even by Brontë standards.

- 'wretched, wretched mistake!' is a passionate utterance and rare use of repetition, non-sentence, strong language and exclamation mark by a JA heroine. Likewise Darcy saying 'Good God!', and the several uses of 'Oh!'

- Darcy with 'brow contracted, his air gloomy' is reminiscent of the most Byronic of Romantic hero stereotypes.

- We know that E. and Darcy dare to stand up to Lady C., which argues strong feeling.

- We know at every point in the novel what E. is experiencing, and some of her feelings run deep and are painful: e.g. embarrassment towards her mother,

disappointment for her father, shame for Lydia, concern about Jane, disapproval of Charlotte, i.e. a wide range of feelings for discerning readers to appreciate if they are sensitive enough.

B   Whole-novel questions

1 **What importance does Mr Collins have in the whole of *Pride and Prejudice*?**

Top band descriptors

- AO1 use of appropriate critical vocabulary and technically fluent expression/ always relevant with a very sharp focus on task.
- AO3 perceptive consideration of some different interpretations of texts with sharp evaluation of their strengths and weaknesses
- AO4 excellent understanding of a range of contextual factors with specific, detailed links between context/texts/task

Possible content

Comment might be made on Collins's comic role; on the way he reveals the characters of Mr Bennet, E. and Charlotte; on the way he is used to reveal attitudes to social class; as a negative representation of the church; as part of the love interest for E. as a foil to Darcy; as part of Austen's design to show that her heroine will only marry for love; as a contrast to Darcy; as a vehicle for irony; to reveal different attitudes to marriage; as a plot device to bring Darcy and E. together at Hunsford etc.

2 **Examine the novel's presentation of the distinctions and relations between different social groups.**

Possible plan

- Social scale narrow: lower to middle country gentry plus Londoners; income from land, trade, church or army.
- Importance of property and landowning, and therefore of independence; biographical as well as literary importance to JA.
- No servants are characterised and rarely even mentioned; not believed relevant for the moral and linguistic issues dealt with.
- Aristocratic figures mocked and seen to be setting a bad example, i.e. Lady C.
- Social satire through differentiation of use of language within the gentry.
- Clergy (another biographical relevance) always a target in JA, e.g. Mr Elton and Dr Grant in addition to Mr Collins; they ironically personify deadly sins of pride (and gluttony) and are hypocritical and uncharitable, not practising what they preach.
- Rising mercantile class represented by Gardiners; initially despised by Bingleys, Darcy and Lady C. but shown to have integrity and manners despite being nouveau riche through trade, and Darcy comes to accept and respect them.

- Real hierarchy applied in P&P is one of moral meritocracy not of amount or source of wealth, which makes E. — 'a gentleman's daughter' — better than Lady C. and the unpretentious and sensible Charlotte better than the affected and insincere Bingley women.

3 'In *Pride and Prejudice*, marriage is presented primarily as an economic arrangement.' How far and in what ways do you agree with this view?

Top band descriptors

- AO1 answers should be fluent and well constructed, showing a creative engagement with the text. Candidates should demonstrate detailed knowledge of marriages and attitudes to marriage in *Pride and Prejudice*, selecting telling illustrative material and using appropriate terminology with confidence.
- AO2 essays should analyse with confidence ways in which Austen presents marriage, considering the effectiveness of aspects such as narrative voice, dialogue, irony and structure.
- AO3 answers should offer a coherently argued view which is usefully informed by the interpretations of other readers. Candidates may make helpful comparisons with additional appropriate texts, e.g. other novels by Austen.
- AO4 answers should show informed insight into the importance of contextual issues such as the role of women and the nature of marriage in the society in which the novel is set.

4 'Irony is central to the meaning and effects of *Pride and Prejudice*.' How far and in what ways do you find this to be the case?

Top band descriptors

- AO1 answers should be fluent and well constructed, showing a creative engagement with the text. Candidates should develop a confident understanding of the term 'irony', and will use a working definition in their answers, whether or not this is explicitly stated; they may draw on the study texts recommended for section B in their explanations/definitions. Essays will select telling illustrative material and use appropriate terminology with confidence.
- AO2 essays should analyse with confidence ways in which Austen uses irony in the novel, considering the effectiveness of aspects such as narrative voice, dialogue, humour and situation.
- AO3 answers should offer a coherently argued view that is usefully informed by the interpretations of other readers. Candidates may make helpful comparisons with additional appropriate texts, e.g. other novels by Austen.
- AO4 answers should show informed insight into the importance of contextual issues such as the conventions surrounding the use of irony in the novel.

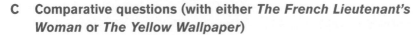

C Comparative questions (with either *The French Lieutenant's Woman* or *The Yellow Wallpaper*)

1 'Female characters are often represented as being constrained by their societies.' Explore the presentation of female characters in the light of this statement.

In your response you should focus on *Pride and Prejudice* to establish your argument, and you should refer to the second text you have read to support and develop your line of argument.

Responses are likely to include reference to the following in establishing an argument using *Pride and Prejudice*:

- their interpretation of the way female characters are represented
- the constraints that may be placed on them and the extent to which these constraints are presented as meaningful
- the way behaviour is described, with close examination of language devices
- an examination of the term 'by their societies': what this means and the extent to which it is a fair observation
- a comparison of the behaviour of different female characters and the way they respond in different ways to the constraints allegedly put on them

2 'There is always a huge contrast between the behaviour of men and women.' Using *Pride and Prejudice*, Chapter 19, p. 104 as your starting point from '"You are too hasty, sir," she cried' to '"as would be consistent with the true delicacy of the female character"' at the bottom of p. 105, explore the presentation of the behaviour of men and women.

In your response you should focus on *Pride and Prejudice* to establish your argument, and you should refer to the second text you have read to support and develop your line of argument.

Responses are likely to include reference to the following in establishing an argument using *Pride and Prejudice*:

- their interpretation of the way male and female characters are represented
- comparisons of the way the behaviour of men and women is shown
- based on the extract, Elizabeth's measured and assertive behaviour in rebuffing Collins's advances
- based on the extract, an exploration of the pompous nature of Collins
- a consideration of the subtleties and ironies in the way Jane Austen presents character and situation
- ways in which the reader is invited to respond
- the way behaviour is described, with close examination of language devices

Sample essays

Below are two sample essays of different types written by different students. Both of them have been assessed as falling within the top band. You can judge them against the Assessment Objectives for this text for your exam board and decide on the mark you think each deserves and why. You may also be able to see ways in which each could be improved in terms of content and style.

Sample essay 1: passage-based

Remind yourself of Chapter 16, from the arrival of Wickham. How does Austen present Elizabeth and Wickham and the relationship between them here?

The dialogue between the George Wickham and Elizabeth Bennet dominates the chapter and gives the impression that they only had interest in each other, the other guests at the party simply providing a backdrop to the beginning of their relationship.

Suspense has already prepared the reader and Elizabeth for the advent of Wickham at the Philips's house, since he was invited previously and Elizabeth is expecting him. He is late to arrive, and has been prepared for as a contrast to the insufferable Collins, rambling on about Rosings, and 'the broad-faced, stuffy uncle Phillips [sic], breathing port wine'. Elizabeth is starved of male company generally, being one of five sisters with a reclusive father. She is now so bored that she is in the mood to find any other male attractive by comparison to those already in the room, and officers were generally expected to be dashing, charming and gentlemanly. Wickham chooses to sit by Elizabeth, immediately winning her good opinion by such flattery, which he extends by preferring to continue to talk to her rather than play whist. We get the impression that he is a lady's man and knows how to charm them. He has the ability to converse easily, so different from Collins.

The relationship becomes more intimate when Wickham brings up the subject of Darcy; he is satisfying both Elizabeth's curiosity and her prejudice, and she is also flattered in the confidence Wickham appears to be placing in her by broaching such a delicate matter. She plays into his hands by being 'unwilling to let the subject drop' (which incidentally reveals a fascination with Darcy which the reader appreciates even if she doesn't) and her naivety allows her to be manipulated by someone adept at steering things his own way. By admitting to Wickham that she finds Darcy 'very disagreeable' she is encouraging Wickham to take further liberties with her and against Darcy. She is led into breaking the rules of etiquette whereby one does not gossip with strangers about a third person in polite society. Wickham is very correct, carefully addressing her as 'Miss Bennet' and using a flawlessly educated style, which seduces Elizabeth, who is very critical of misuse of language, into believing his morals are of an equally high standard. His claim that he has no right to give an opinion as he could not be a fair judge gains him more credit for correct behaviour, and is a screen for the fact that he does go on to give a very strong negative impression of Darcy. His apparent refusal to be drawn provokes Elizabeth into displaying one of her moral flaws, which is to exaggerate and express herself in extremes:

'He is not at all liked in Hertfordshire. Everybody is disgusted with his pride. You will not find him more favourably spoken of by anyone.'

He fishes for information which she freely gives, as to how long Darcy might be intending to stay in the neighbourhood. She does not realise that he is simply using her, both to boost his own reputation in the community as a worthy person and to attract sympathy as a victim of Darcy's arrogance, 'ill-usage' and 'scandalous' behaviour. They are as if placed in a pair of scales, and Wickham's rise inevitably links to Darcy's fall in the local estimation. Wickham's praise of Darcy's father as 'one of the best men that ever breathed' prevents any suspicion that he may have a grudge against the family or that he is incapable of appreciation of the good qualities of others, making his condemnation of Darcy all the more damning. Elizabeth's sense of justice is outraged by Wickham's claim that he was deprived of the living due to him. Her language — exclamations and questions — shows how shocked she is. He dismisses his detractor's accusations towards him of 'extravagance, imprudence' — exactly those attributes that will turn out to be justified — as 'anything or nothing' and makes the focus fall on the fact that Darcy hates him. That Elizabeth has lost her ability to separate the content of the utterance from the attractiveness of the utterer is made clear when we are told 'Elizabeth honoured him for such feelings, and thought him handsomer than ever as he expressed them' and that she thought that his 'very countenance may vouch to [his] being amiable'. It is serious when a Jane Austen heroine loses her reason and ability to judge. Once she has mentioned Darcy's pride he harps on the word, using 'pride' or 'proud' eight times in a few lines. This reiteration and the plausible answer he seems to have for every question create the impression that he must be telling the truth and giving an accurate assessment of Darcy.

Wickham comes out of this chapter as a skilful womaniser and social manipulator, someone who uses 'intelligible gallantry'; Elizabeth as inexperienced in the ways of men and the world and too trusting of her own belief in her ability to judge people. A relationship seems to have been formed that would lead those who see them together and Elizabeth herself to think that he has formed at attachment to her. Because Wickham has taken notice of her exclusively, behaving in exactly the opposite way towards her from Darcy at the Meryton assembly, where he publicly humiliated her, Elizabeth has feelings of gratitude for her restored pride as well as other reasons to like her saviour, who has told her everything she wanted to hear. One wonders whether Wickham has done his homework and made enquiries which led him to believe that Elizabeth might be susceptible to his charms and a useful ally against Darcy. He also praises Meryton and its society, which is again in contrast to Darcy's expressed derogatory views on small country towns and their inhabitants. He goes on to describe Lady Catherine in a way Elizabeth can recognise, so she is convinced that Wickham is 'rational', which is an important concept for her and theme for the novel. Being rational is protection against being misled by emotion into forming misjudgements, but ironically it does not protect Elizabeth in this case.

This is an important chapter as it shows Elizabeth being fallible and over-confident, guilty of both pride and a prejudice, which will cause trouble for herself, Darcy and her family later on, when her reluctance to tell them what she has learnt about Wickham exposes Lydia to risk and all the Bennets to social catastrophe. She confuses the hero and the villain in the story from this moment, and makes allowances for one young man and not the other until the truth is revealed much later in Darcy's letter.

Sample essay 2: general question

'In *Pride and Prejudice*, marriage is presented primarily as an economic arrangement.' How far and in what ways do you agree with this view?

The novel's opening sentence is famously about money and marriage, and many critics have dismissed Jane Austen's novels as being only about the mercenary matches, the selling of virginity, and the 'amorous effects of "brass"' as Auden put it in his poem. They are in fact about deeper issues than just finding a partner, as in a shallow romantic fiction, since considerations of judgement and morality are explored, with marriage as only one example of a relationship and social contract, and one that is presented as being about more than just a convenient economic arrangement.

Marriage was viewed differently in those days, when it was common for cousins to marry to keep property in the family and perpetuate dynasties, and marrying only for love was regarded as something whimsical at best and feckless at worst. There are examples of bad marriages in this and other Austen novels to warn the reader of the consequences of marrying for the wrong reasons and to reveal Austen's views on what the basis of marriage should not be, including purely physical attraction. Mr Bennet made the mistake of marrying Mrs Bennet for her body with no regard to her mind, or lack of it, and has not only regretted it ever since but has caused unfortunate genes to be passed down to some of his daughters, and all of them to suffer from the lack of an appropriate role model for a mother. The lack of affection and respect in the Bennet marriage, the lack of passion in the Hurst marriage, and Charlotte's need to keep poultry and find other ways to divert herself from being married to Mr Collins all prove that Austen did not recommend that marriage should be primarily based on economic need.

Only for the unpleasant or stupid characters in the novel does the definition of marriage as an economic arrangement apply, and for this they are ridiculed or criticised by the heroine or narrative voice, beginning with the satirical opening sentence. Mrs Bennet wants to get her daughters off her hands and use them to bring some prosperity into the family and she doesn't care whether the pairings are suitable; Wickham marries Lydia because he is paid to, and Lydia will marry anyone in order to get a household of her own; Lady Catherine wants her daughter to marry her nephew to keep Pemberley in the family; Mr Collins chooses a wife because he is told to do so and is not looking for a soulmate but an assistant; Charlotte accepts him because it's the best offer she is likely to get and she needs financial security; Caroline Bingley has nothing in common with Darcy but likes the idea of becoming mistress of a grand estate.

However, the characters we are asked to identify with and approve of take a different view of marriage, one that involves shared interests and attitudes. The Gardiners are a responsible, respectable and civilised couple, unlike the Philipses, and their kindness and sensitivity to Jane and Elizabeth validate their marriage as a successful one in which money is not particularly abundant but they have enough to support their large family's needs, unlike the Bennets. Mr Bennet, who is morally dubious only in some areas, strongly disapproves of the idea that Elizabeth should marry someone as inappropriate as Mr Collins, who is not a 'sensible man', even though it would have been a good economic arrangement to secure Longbourn from the entail.

Economic factors cannot be completely ignored, as marrying beneath oneself and ending up in poverty is not to be recommended in a society without means of support other than a good income and family resources, and it is foolish and irrational to think money, property and status do not matter. These factors were particularly important for men, as they had to provide for their future wife and children at a time when women had no profession or income and could contribute only their dowries to the match. However, marriages out of one's social or intellectual level do not work in Jane Austen, however much money is available. Elizabeth jokes that she fell in love with Darcy after seeing his estate, but in fact it was what Pemberley showed her about the values and tastes of its owner that really mattered.

The novel makes it clear that a couple should be able to appreciate the same things. Jane and Bingley's marriage will be a dull one because neither of them are very sensitive or perceptive, but it will be a happy one because they are remarkably similar in being undemanding, undemonstrative, amiable and capable of affection. The Wickham marriage, by contrast, is likely to end disastrously when Lydia tires of the novelty of being Mrs Wickham and starts to look around for someone else to practise her charms on, or when Wickham finds her empty-headedness tiresome, since he is actually much more intelligent and sophisticated than her. Lydia is already begging for money from Elizabeth by the end of the novel, so we know that in their case there is no sound economic basis to allow their relationship to flourish, and instead they are likely to come to resent each other's lack of wealth and having to live in debt, constantly moving on to avoid creditors, or in increasingly straitened circumstances, which will not suit them at all.

Elizabeth and Darcy both ignore representations and expectations from others, based on economic criteria, as to whom they should marry, and choose their mate according to the way in which they can teach and learn from each other, their shared appreciation of nature and beauty, their respect for each other's intelligence and independent spirit. The mutual physical attraction and Darcy's wealth are the icing on the cake of compatibility, which is the first and foremost requirement for a successful marriage in Austen's view.

Further study

Jane Austen is one of the most popular novelists in the English language and has a large following of devoted fans, including those known as 'Janeites', who have contributed to a virtual industry in the production of books and materials about her life and works. Much of this is adulatory rather than critical, and some is speculative (note the recent fictional reconstruction of her love life in the film *Becoming Jane*), so it is important to be selective. The following works have been found to be useful to literature students and have stood the test of time.

Books

Austen-Leigh, J. (1870) *A Memoir of Jane Austen*, Oxford University Press (available as a free download from www.gutenberg.org/etext/17797).

Austen-Leigh, W. (1913) *Jane Austen: Her Life and Letters* (available as a free download from www.gutenberg.org/etext/22536).

Butler, M. (1988) *Jane Austen and the War of Ideas*, Clarendon Press.

Cecil, D. (2000) *A Portrait of Jane Austen*, Penguin.

Chapman, R. W. (ed.) (1955) *Jane Austen: Letters 1796–1817*, Oxford University Press.

Copeland, E. and McMaster, J. (eds) (1997) *The Cambridge Companion to Jane Austen*, Cambridge University Press.

Craik, W. (1965) *Jane Austen: The Six Novels*, Methuen.

Forster, E. M. (2005) *Aspects of the Novel*, Penguin.

Gilbert, S. and Gubar, S. (2000) *The Madwoman in the Attic*, Yale University Press.

Lascelles, M. (1995) *Jane Austen and her Art*, Continuum.

Page, N. (1972) *The Language of Jane Austen*, Oxford University Press.

Phillipps, K. (1970) *Jane Austen's English*, Deutsch.

Southam, B. (ed.) (1995) *Jane Austen: the Critical Heritage Vols 1 & 2*, Routledge.

Tomalin, C. (2000) *Jane Austen: A Life*, Penguin.

Watt, I. (ed.) (1963) *Jane Austen: Twentieth Century Views*, Prentice Hall.

Woolf, V. (2002) *A Room of One's Own*, Penguin.

Woolf, V. (2002) *The Common Reader*, Harvest.

Wright, A. (1972) *Jane Austen's Novels: A Study in Structure*, Penguin.

Essays

Eagleton, T. (2005) 'Walter Scott and Jane Austen', in Malden, M. (ed.) *The English Novel: An Introduction*, Blackwell, pp. 94–122. Most of the text of this key chapter can be found on Google Books at books.google.co.uk/books (a more complete URL cannot be given because of the way the Google site includes session cookies in the address bar).

Harding, D. (1940) 'Regulated Hatred: An Aspect of the Work of Jane Austen', in Watt, I. (ed.) *Jane Austen: Twentieth Century Views*, Prentice Hall.

Hough, G. (1970) 'Narrative and Dialogue in Jane Austen', in the author's *Selected Essays*, Cambridge University Press.

Leavis, Q. (1941–44) 'A Critical Theory of Jane Austen's Writings', in the author's *Collected Essays*, Cambridge University Press.

Film/television productions

1938: television series starring Curigwen Lewis and Andrew Osborn, adapted by Michael Barry.

1940: film version directed by Robert Z. Leonard, starring Greer Garson and Laurence Olivier, adapted by Aldous Huxley. Greer Garson claimed that the costumes were recycled from *Gone with the Wind* and therefore completely anachronistic. In this version Lady Catherine eventually agrees to the marriage. Slapstick comic scenes are inserted.

1952: television series directed by Campbell Logan, starring Daphne Slater and Peter Cushing, adapted by Cedric Wallis.

1958: television series starring Jane Downs and Alan Badel; the script was recycled from the 1952 version.

1967: television series directed by Joan Craft, starring Celia Bannerman and Lewis Fiander, adapted by Nemone Lethbridge.

1980: television series directed by Cyril Coke, starring Elizabeth Garvie and David Rintoul, adapted by Fay Weldon.

1995: television series directed by Matthew Langton, starring Jennifer Ehle and Colin Firth, adapted by Andrew Davies. This was the celebrated production in which Colin Firth scandalised the more staid 'Janeites' by emerging from the Pemberley lake in a wet shirt and tight white breeches.

2004: 'Bollywood' version *Bride & Prejudice*, directed by Gurinder Chadham, starring Aishwarya Rai, Martin Henderson and Daniel Gillies, the action is transferred to present-day India.

2005: film version directed by Joe Wright, starring Keira Knightley and Matthew MacFadyen, adapted by Deborah Moggach; many viewers consider the approach to be too modern, and Keira Knightley to be too pretty.

Internet resources

A Google search for 'Jane Austen' returns 6,410,000 results. 'Pride and Prejudice' gives a mere 3,700,000. It would be more than a lifetime's work to go through all these; what follows is a selection of sites that are useful and seem to have broadly reliable information.

As a starting point, a full (searchable) e-text of the novel is available from Project Gutenberg at www.gutenberg.org/etext/1342. An illustrated and annotated hypertext is available at www.pemberley.com/janeinfo/pridprej.html, an outstanding site with many useful features and links.

Another searchable e-text is at: www.online-literature.com/austen/prideprejudice/

A useful bibliography of criticism can be found at users.ox.ac.uk/~engf0047/Austen.htm

The Jane Austen Society of North America publishes an excellent website with an online journal, Persuasions, dealing with all of Austen's works: www.jasna.org/

Sequels

An extraordinary feature of the Jane Austen phenomenon is the large number of works of fiction, in prose, verse and drama, inspired by her novels and parasitic upon them. There are more than 20 sequels, prequels and alternative renderings of *Pride and Prejudice*, some by recognised novelists; perhaps the most prestigious is *Pemberley* by Emma Tennant (1993). At least eight have been published since 2002, so the trend shows no sign of abating. A reasonably full list, with discussion, may be found at: www.erasofelegance.com/arts/literature/janebooks.html

Outstanding teaching and learning 14-19

Bradley Lightbody